Party Cakes & MORE

FUN FOODS FOR KIDS

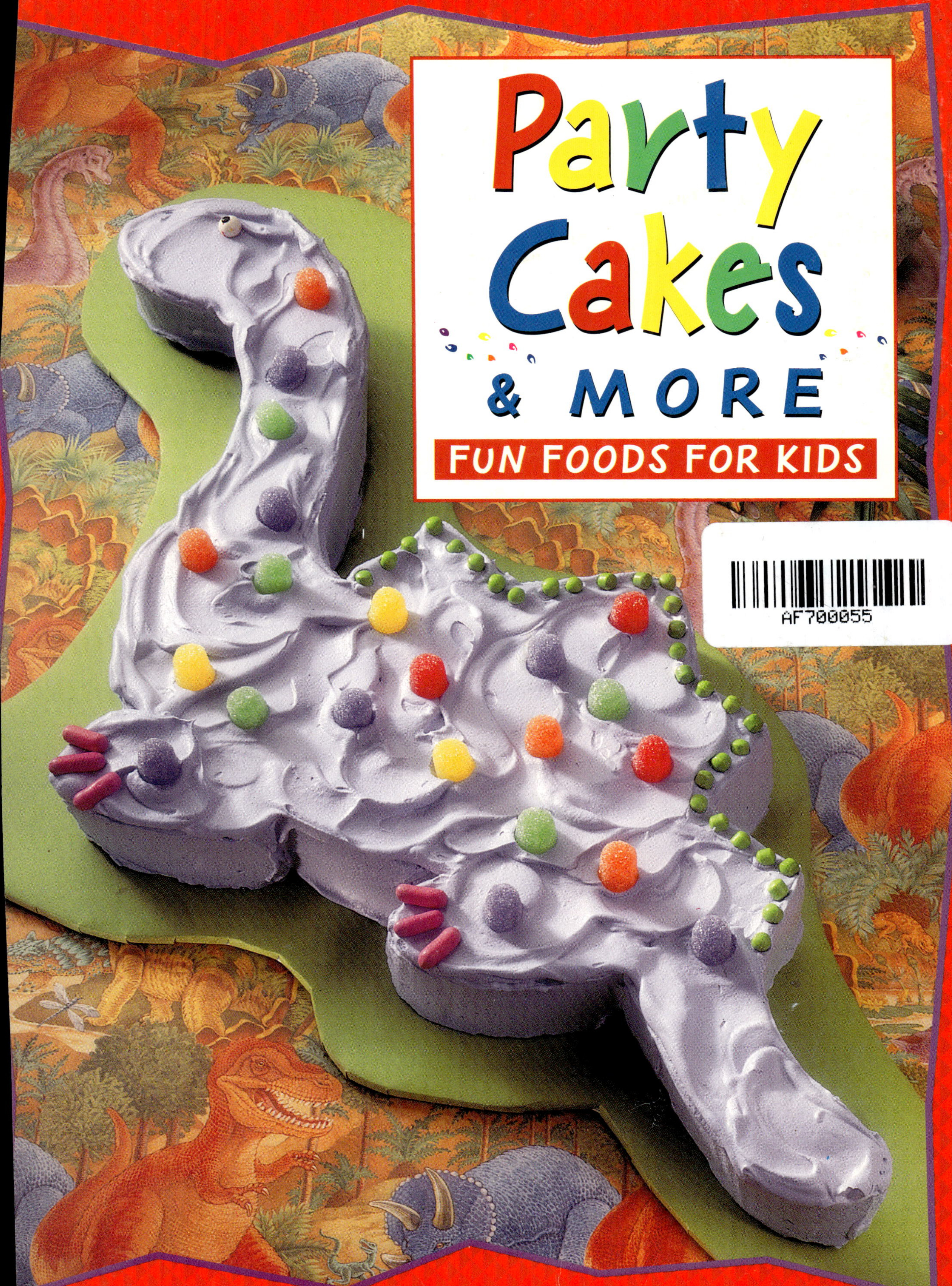

Party Cakes & More

Contents

Basic Recipes

Creamy Decorator's Frosting

Makes about 5 cups

1½ cups vegetable shortening
1½ teaspoons lemon, coconut, almond or peppermint extract
7½ cups sifted powdered sugar
⅓ cup milk

Beat shortening and extract in large bowl with electric mixer on medium speed until fluffy. Slowly add ½ of sugar, ½ cup at a time, beating well after each addition. Beat in milk. Add remaining sugar; beat 1 minute more until smooth and fluffy.* Store in refrigerator. (Frosting may be used for frosting cake and/or piping decorations.)

**If frosting seems too soft for piping roses or other detailed flowers or borders, refrigerate for a few hours. Refrigerating frosting usually gives better results, but you may also try stirring in additional sifted sugar, ¼ cup at a time, until desired consistency.*

Note: This frosting also works well as the base frosting on a cake. Thin frosting by adding a little more milk.

Fluffy White Frosting

Makes about 2 cups frosting

1 container (16 ounces) vanilla frosting
¾ cup marshmallow creme

Combine frosting and marshmallow creme in medium bowl; mix well.

Creamy White Frosting

Makes enough to fill and frost 2 (8-inch) round or square cake layers or frost 1 (13×9-inch) cake

½ cup vegetable shortening
6 cups sifted powdered sugar, divided
3 tablespoons milk
2 teaspoons clear vanilla extract
Additional milk*

**For thinner frosting, use more milk and for thicker frosting use less milk.*

Beat shortening in large bowl with electric mixer at medium speed until fluffy. Gradually beat in 3 cups sugar until well blended and smooth. Carefully beat in 3 tablespoons milk and vanilla. Gradually beat in remaining 3 cups sugar, adding more milk, 1 teaspoon at a time, as needed for good spreading consistency. Store in refrigerator.

Fudge Frosting

Makes enough to fill and frost 2 (8-inch) round or square cake layers or frost 1 (13×9-inch) cake

24 large marshmallows, halved
⅔ cup semisweet chocolate chips
½ cup vegetable shortening
½ cup water
5 cups sifted powdered sugar
3 teaspoons vanilla

Place marshmallows, chocolate, shortening and water in 1½-quart saucepan. Cook over low heat until melted and smooth, stirring constantly. Remove from heat; let stand 5 minutes. Gradually beat in sugar and vanilla with electric mixer at medium speed about 6 minutes or until mixture starts to lose gloss. Use frosting immediately.

Base Frosting

Makes about 2 cups

3 cups powdered sugar, sifted
½ cup vegetable shortening
¼ cup milk
½ teaspoon vanilla
Additional milk

Combine sugar, shortening, ¼ cup milk and vanilla in large bowl. Beat with electric mixer on medium speed until smooth. Add more milk, 1 teaspoon at a time, until frosting is a thin consistency. Use frosting immediately.

White Cake

Makes 2 (8-inch) round or square cake layers or 1 (13×9-inch) cake

2½ cups all-purpose flour
1¾ cups sugar
3 teaspoons baking powder
¼ teaspoon salt
1½ cups milk
½ cup vegetable shortening
2 teaspoons vanilla
4 egg whites

Preheat oven to 350°F. Combine flour, sugar, baking powder and salt in large bowl. Add milk, shortening and vanilla. Beat with electric mixer on low speed 30 seconds or until well blended, scraping side of bowl once. Beat on high speed 2 minutes, scraping side of bowl occasionally. Add egg whites; beat 2 minutes more, scraping bowl once. Grease and flour bottoms and sides of 2 (8-inch) round or square cake pans or 1 (13×9-inch) cake pan. Pour batter evenly into pans.

Bake 30 to 35 minutes for 8-inch round or square cakes or 35 to 40 minutes for 13×9-inch cake. Cakes are done when toothpick inserted into centers comes out clean. Cool in pans on wire racks 10 minutes. Loosen sides of cake layers from pans with knife or metal spatula. Remove to wire racks; cool completely.

Chocolate Cake

Makes 2 (8-inch) round or square cake layers or 1 (13×9-inch) cake

2 cups sugar
1⅔ cups all-purpose flour
½ cup unsweetened cocoa powder
1 teaspoon baking powder
½ teaspoon baking soda
¼ teaspoon salt
1 cup buttermilk
½ cup vegetable shortening
1 teaspoon vanilla
3 eggs

Preheat oven to 350°F. Combine sugar, flour, cocoa, baking powder, baking soda and salt in large bowl. Add buttermilk, shortening and vanilla. Beat with electric mixer on low speed 30 seconds or until well blended, scraping side of bowl once. Beat on high speed 2 minutes more, scraping side of bowl occasionally. Add eggs; beat 2 minutes more, scraping bowl once. Grease and flour 2 (8-inch) round or square cake pans or 1 (13×9-inch) cake pan. Pour batter evenly into pans.

Bake 30 to 35 minutes for 8-inch round or square cakes or 35 to 40 minutes for 13×9-inch cake. Cakes are done when toothpick inserted into centers comes out clean. Cool in pans on wire racks 10 minutes. Loosen sides of cake layers from pans with knife or metal spatula. Remove to wire racks; cool completely.

Note: To prepare 10- and 12-inch cake layers, see Note on page 5.

Yellow Cake

Makes 2 (8-inch) round or square cake layers or 1 (13×9-inch) cake

2½ cups all-purpose flour
1¾ cups sugar
2½ teaspoons baking powder
¼ teaspoon salt
1⅓ cups milk
½ cup butter or margarine, softened
2 teaspoons vanilla
3 eggs

Preheat oven to 350°F. Combine flour, sugar, baking powder and salt in large bowl. Add milk, butter and vanilla. Beat with electric mixer on low speed 30 seconds or until well blended, scraping side of bowl once. Beat on high speed 2 minutes more, scraping bowl often. Add eggs; beat 2 minutes more, scraping bowl once. Grease and flour 2 (8-inch) round or square cake pans or 1 (13×9-inch) cake pan. Pour batter evenly into pans. Bake 30 to 35 minutes for 8-inch round or square cakes or 35 to 40 minutes for 13×9-inch cake. Cakes are done when toothpick inserted into centers comes out clean. Cool in pans on wire racks 10 minutes. Loosen sides of cake layers from pans with knife or metal spatula. Remove to wire racks; cool completely.

Note: To prepare 10- and 12-inch layers, double ingredients and prepare batter as directed. Grease and flour 1 (10-inch) and 1 (12-inch) cake pan. Pour batter into cake pans, filling each half full. (You will need more batter in 12-inch pan.) Bake 35 to 40 minutes for 10-inch cake and 40 to 45 minutes for 12-inch cake. Cakes are done when toothpick inserted into centers comes out clean. Cool as directed. Repeat procedure with another double batch of cake batter for second 10- and 12-inch cake layers.

Butter Cookie Dough

Makes about 3 cups dough

¾ cup butter, softened
¼ cup granulated sugar
¼ cup packed light brown sugar
1 egg yolk
1¾ cups all-purpose flour
¾ teaspoon baking powder
⅛ teaspoon salt

1. Combine butter, granulated sugar, brown sugar and egg yolk in medium bowl. Add flour, baking powder and salt; mix well.

2. Cover; refrigerate about 4 hours or until firm.

Unforgettable Birthday Cakes

Corky the Clown

Makes 16 to 18 servings

CAKES & FROSTINGS
1 (9-inch) square cake
1 (9-inch) round cake
3 cups Buttercream Frosting (recipe follows)*
1 recipe Base Frosting (page 3) (optional)
Orange, yellow and pink paste food coloring

DECORATIONS & EQUIPMENT
1 (19×13-inch) cake board, covered
Pastry bags, medium writing tip and star tip
Assorted candies

**Color 3/4 cup frosting orange, 1/2 cup yellow and 1/4 cup pink; reserve 1 1/2 cups white frosting.*

1. Trim tops and sides of cakes. Cut square cake as shown in diagram 1.

2. Position pieces on prepared cake board as shown in diagram 2, connecting pieces with some of the Buttercream Frosting.

3. Frost entire cake with Base Frosting to seal in crumbs, if desired.

4. Frost face with Buttercream Frosting. Using writing tip and pink frosting, pipe mouth.

5. Frost bow tie and top of hat with yellow frosting as shown in photo. Frost hat with some of the orange frosting. Using star tip and orange frosting, pipe design on hat and bow tie. Arrange assorted candies as shown.

Buttercream Frosting

6 cups powdered sugar, sifted and divided
3/4 cup butter or margarine, softened
1/4 cup shortening
6 to 8 tablespoons milk, divided
1 teaspoon vanilla

Combine 3 cups powdered sugar, butter, shortening, 4 tablespoons milk and vanilla in large bowl. Beat with electric mixer until smooth. Add remaining powdered sugar; beat until light and fluffy, adding more milk, 1 tablespoon at a time, as needed for good spreading consistency.

Makes about 3 1/2 cups

Corky the Clown

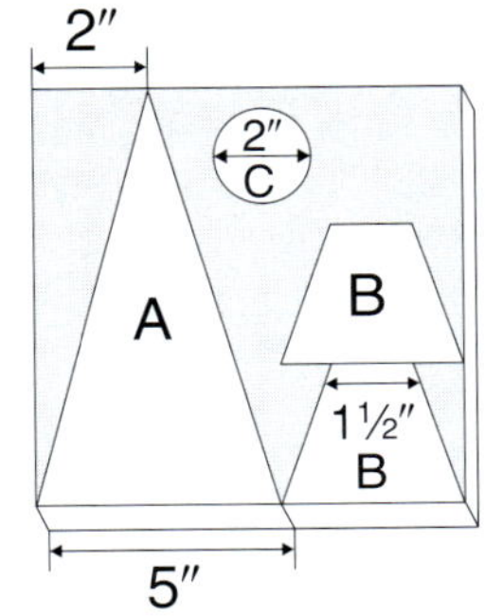

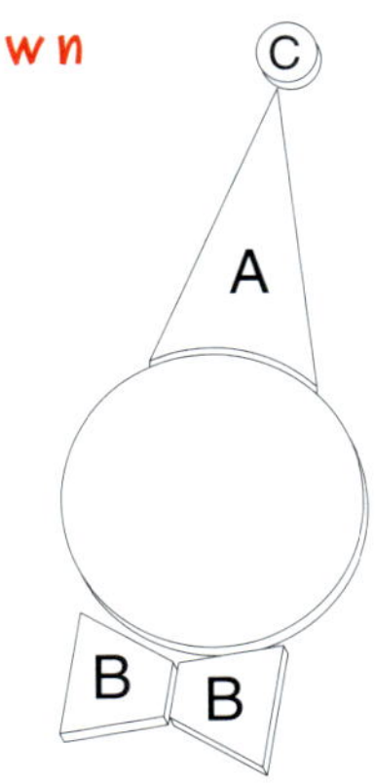

Balloon Cake

With this eye-catching cake, guests at a birthday party or other celebration can have their balloons and eat them too. Decorate the balloons in the favorite colors of the guest of honor.

Makes 16 to 20 servings

CAKE & FROSTINGS

1 (13×9-inch) cake
1 recipe Creamy Decorator's Frosting (page 2)
Blue, green and yellow paste food coloring
1 to 2 tablespoons milk
1 recipe Creamy White Frosting (page 3)

EQUIPMENT

1 (19×13-inch) cake board, covered
4 decorating bags with couplers
Tips: Numbers 2, 4 and 7

1. Trim top and sides of cake. Place cake on prepared cake board.

2. To tint Creamy Decorator's Frosting, tint ¼ cup blue, ¼ cup green, ¼ cup yellow and reserve 1¼ cups for white frosting. Thin remaining Creamy Decorator's Frosting with milk, adding 1 teaspoon at a time, until frosting is a thin consistency.

3. Frost top and sides of cake with thinned frosting to seal in crumbs. Frost again with Creamy White Frosting. Smooth frosting on top and sides.

4. To make balloons, start on left side of cake in center and pipe line in balloon shape with blue frosting and number 4 tip.

5. Pipe dots to completely fill in balloon outline with same frosting and tip as shown in photo 1. (Pipe dots over outline as well.) Repeat to make green and yellow balloons as shown in photo, switching tip with couplers.

6. Carefully smooth surface of dots with damp, not wet, tip of knife as shown in photo 2.

7. Pipe line for center balloon with blue frosting and number 4 tip, piping string straight down. Pipe other strings angled to meet center string with yellow and green frostings, switching tip with couplers.

8. To pipe bow, start at center where strings meet and pipe line in figure 8 with blue and green frostings and number 4 tip.

9. Pipe 1 word in desired writing on each balloon with reserved white frosting and number 2 tip.

10. Pipe bottom and top dot borders with white frosting and switching to number 7 tip. Pipe 3 dots at each corner as border accents with blue, green and yellow frostings and number 4 tip.

Balloon Cake

1

2

Gummy Purple Dinosaur Cake

Of course, dinosaurs can come in other colors, too.

Makes 12 to 16 servings

1 tub (8 ounces) COOL WHIP® Whipped Topping, thawed
Few drops blue and red food coloring
1 baked 13×9-inch cake, any flavor except angel food, cooled
Gumdrops
Assorted small candies

TINT whipped topping purple with blue and red food colorings in small bowl with wire whisk.

CUT cake as shown in diagram 1.

USING small amount of whipped topping to hold pieces together, arrange cake on serving tray as shown in diagram 2. Frost cake with remaining whipped topping. Decorate with gumdrops and candies. Serve immediately. Store leftover cake in refrigerator.

Drum Layer Cake

Makes 12 to 16 servings

1 package DUNCAN HINES® Moist Deluxe Cake Mix (any flavor)
1 container DUNCAN HINES® Vanilla Frosting, divided
Green food coloring
Thin pretzel sticks
Candy-coated chocolate pieces
Lollipops

1. Preheat oven to 350°F. Grease and flour two 8-inch round cake pans.

2. Prepare, bake and cool cake following package directions for basic recipe.

3. To assemble, place half the Vanilla frosting in small bowl. Tint with green food coloring; set aside. Place one cake layer on serving plate. Spread with half of untinted Vanilla frosting. Top with second cake layer. Spread green frosting on sides of cake. Spread remaining Vanilla frosting on top of cake. Arrange pretzel sticks and candy-coated chocolates on sides of cake. Place lollipops on top of cake for "drumsticks."

FUN TIP

For brighter green frosting, use paste food colors available from cake decorating and specialty shops.

Gummy Purple Dinosaur Cake

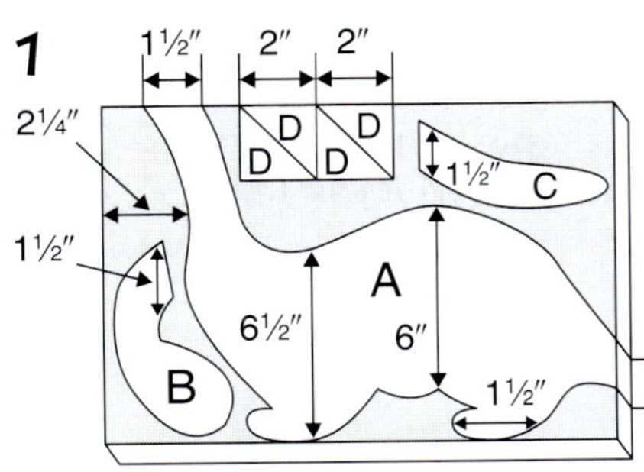

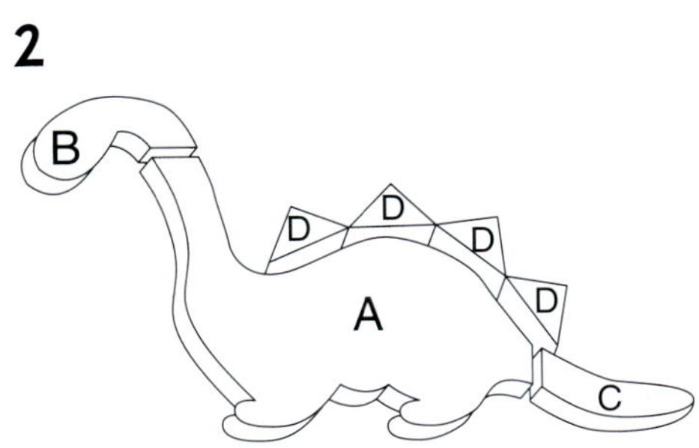

Football Cake

Makes 12 to 16 servings

1 package DUNCAN HINES® Moist Deluxe Devil's Food Cake Mix
¾ cup confectioners' sugar
2 tablespoons shortening
1 tablespoon cold water
1 tablespoon non-dairy powdered creamer
¼ teaspoon vanilla extract
Dash salt
1 container DUNCAN HINES® Chocolate Frosting

1. Preheat oven to 350°F. Grease and flour 10-inch round cake pan. Prepare cake following package directions for basic recipe. Bake at 350°F 45 to 55 minutes or until toothpick inserted in center comes out clean.

2. Combine sugar, shortening, water, creamer, vanilla and salt in small bowl. Beat at medium speed with electric mixer 2 minutes. Add more sugar to thicken or water to thin frosting as needed.

3. Cut cake according to diagrams 1 and 2, removing 2-inch slice from center. Arrange cake as shown in diagram 3. Spread Chocolate frosting on sides and top of cake. Place basketweave tip in pastry bag. Fill with decorator frosting. Pipe laces.

FUN TIP

Make 2 football cakes following package directions for 2 (9-inch) round cake pans.

Flower Garden Cake

Makes 16 to 20 servings

1 package DUNCAN HINES® Moist Deluxe Yellow or Devil's Food Cake Mix
1 container DUNCAN HINES® Vanilla Frosting
Green food coloring
Mini pretzels
½ teaspoon water
1 cup flaked coconut
Narrow green ribbon
Assorted candy suckers

1. Preheat oven to 350°F. Grease and flour 13×9×2-inch pan.

2. Prepare and bake cake following package directions for basic recipe. Cool completely.

3. Tint Vanilla frosting with 3 drops green food coloring. Frost sides and top of cake. Place pretzels upright along top edge to form "fence." Combine water and food coloring in small bowl. Add coconut. Toss with fork until evenly tinted. Sprinkle coconut "grass" over frosting inside pretzel "fence." Tie ribbon bows on each candy sucker stick to form leaves. Arrange assorted sucker "flowers" in "garden."

Football Cake

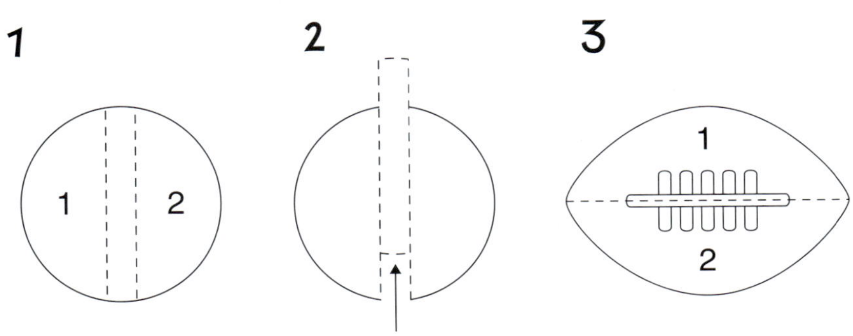

Double Dip Ice Cream Cone Cakes

Serve both cakes for a "double dip," or freeze one for the next occasion.

Makes 12 to 14 servings

1 package (2-layer size) cake mix, any flavor
4 squares BAKER'S® Semi-Sweet Chocolate
¼ cup milk
1 tub (8 ounces) COOL WHIP® Whipped Topping, thawed
Assorted small candies
Multicolored sprinkles
Maraschino cherries

HEAT oven to 350°F.

PREPARE cake mix as directed on package. Divide batter evenly between greased and floured 8-inch round and 8-inch square baking pans. Bake as directed on package. Cool 10 minutes; remove from pans. Cool completely on wire racks.

CUT cakes as shown in diagrams 1 and 2. Assemble pieces on large serving tray as shown in diagrams 3 and 4.

MICROWAVE chocolate and milk in medium microwavable bowl on HIGH 2 minutes or until chocolate is almost melted. Stir until chocolate is completely melted. Cool 20 minutes or until room temperature. Gently stir 1½ cups whipped topping into chocolate with wire whisk until blended.

FROST "cones" with chocolate whipped topping mixture; decorate with candies, if desired. Frost "ice cream" with remaining whipped topping; decorate with sprinkles.

REFRIGERATE until ready to serve. Top with cherries just before serving.

Double Dip Ice Cream Cone Cake

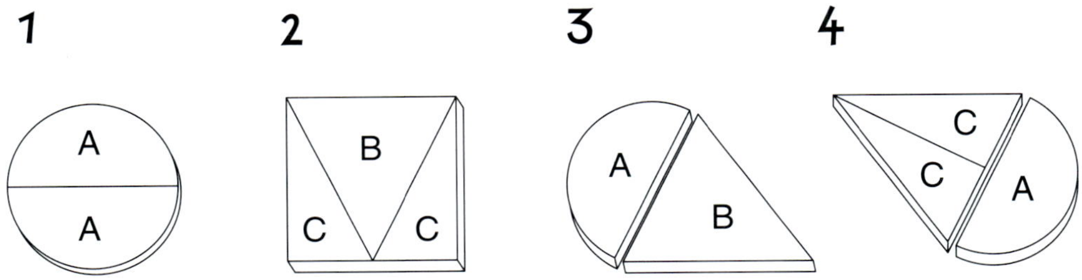

Castle Cake

Make this delightful castle a family project. It's so easy even the youngest members of your kingdom can help decorate it.

Makes 8 to 10 servings

CAKE & FROSTING

1 (8-inch) square cake
1 recipe Creamy White Frosting (page 3)
Yellow and blue paste food coloring
1 to 2 tablespoons milk

DECORATIONS & EQUIPMENT

1 (19×13-inch) cake board, covered
1 (3-inch) peppermint candy stick
¼ cup sliced natural almonds
16 red licorice bites
Tiny multi-colored candies and sprinkles

1. Trim top and sides of cake. Cut cake as shown in diagram 1 with serrated knife, using ruler as guide. Freeze pieces 30 to 45 minutes before frosting.

2. To tint frosting, tint 1½ cups bright yellow and ¼ cup bright blue. Thin remaining frosting with milk, adding 1 teaspoon at a time, until frosting is a thin consistency.

3. Position pieces A, B and C on prepared cake board as shown in diagram 2, connecting with some of the yellow frosting. Frost both sides and tops with thinned frosting to seal in crumbs. Frost again with remaining yellow frosting.

4. Hold piece D in left hand. Starting at the point, carefully spread thinned frosting along the side, using long strokes in the direction away from point until all sides are frosted; frost top. Frost again with blue frosting. Position candy stick and blue piece as shown in photo.

5. Decorate with almonds and remaining candy as shown in photo.

Castle Cake

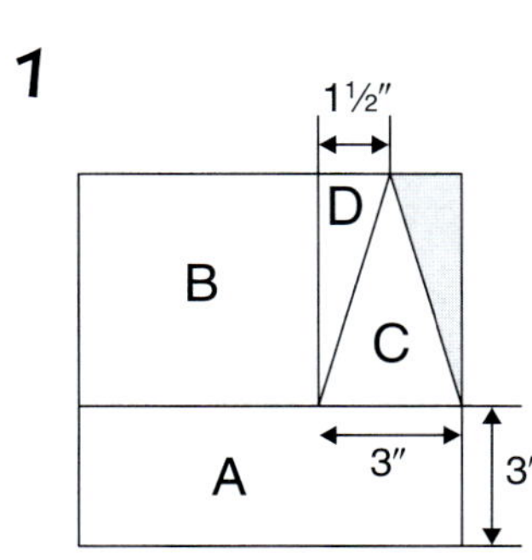

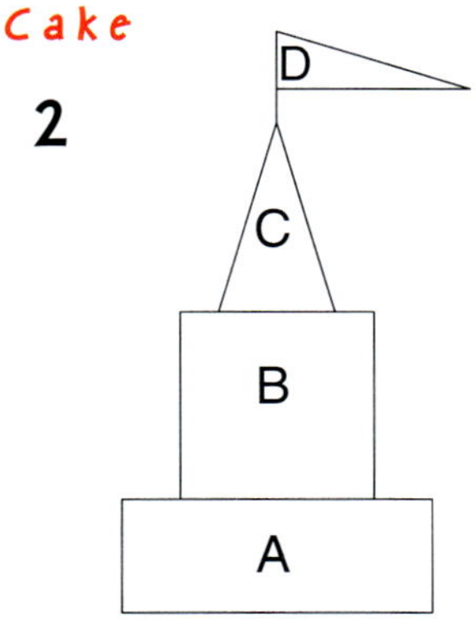

Merry-Go-Round Cake

This makes an ordinary cake into a carousel of fun.

Makes 12 servings

1 package (6-serving size) JELL-O® Instant Pudding and Pie Filling, Vanilla Flavor
1 package (2-layer size) yellow cake mix
4 eggs
1 cup water
¼ cup vegetable oil
⅓ cup BAKER'S® Semi-Sweet Real Chocolate Chips, melted
⅔ cup cold milk
Sprinkles (optional)
Paper carousel roof (directions follow)
3 plastic straws
6 animal crackers

RESERVE ⅓ cup pudding mix. Combine cake mix, remaining pudding mix, eggs, water and oil in large bowl. Beat at low speed of electric mixer just to moisten, scraping sides of bowl often. Beat at medium speed 4 minutes. Pour ½ of the batter into greased and floured 10-inch fluted tube pan. Mix chocolate into remaining batter. Spoon over batter in pan; cut through with spatula in zigzag pattern to marbleize. Bake at 350°F for 50 minutes or until cake tester inserted in center comes out clean. Cool in pan 15 minutes. Remove from pan; finish cooling on rack.

BEAT reserved pudding mix and milk in small bowl until smooth. Spoon over top of cake to glaze. Garnish with sprinkles, if desired.

CUT 10- to 12-inch circle from colored paper; scallop edges, if desired. Make 1 slit to center (diagram 1). Overlap cut edges to form carousel roof; secure with tape (diagram 2). Cut straws in half; arrange on cake with animal crackers. Top with roof.

Prep Time: 30 minutes
Bake Time: 50 minutes

Merry-Go-Round Cake

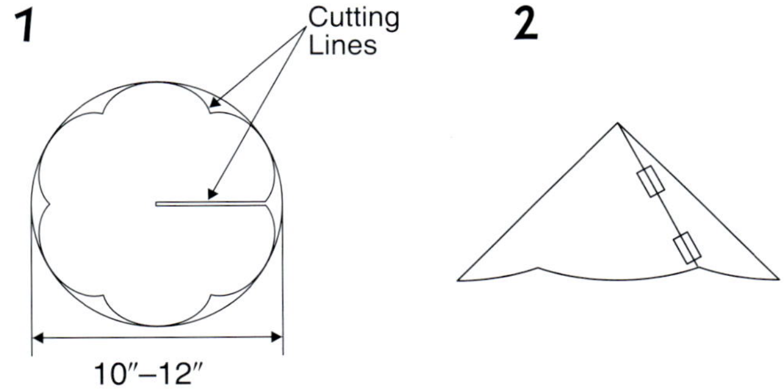

Alphabet Block Cake

Makes 32 to 36 servings

4 (8-inch) square cake layers*

BUTTERCREAM FROSTING
1 cup butter or margarine, softened
⅓ cup shortening
8 cups (2 pounds) powdered sugar, sifted, divided
½ cup plus 2 tablespoons milk, divided
1 teaspoon vanilla
Blue food coloring
Green food coloring
Jelly (your favorite flavor), melted (about 2½ cups)

DECORATIONS & EQUIPMENT
1 (19×14-inch) cake board
Candy-coated chocolate pieces
Ice cream cone-shaped cookie cutter
Pastry bag and medium writing tip
Chocolate sprinkles
Pink colored sugar

**Use your favorite cake recipe or package mix; follow baking instructions for 8-inch square cakes. Two cakes (4 layers) are needed.*

1. Trim tops and edges of cakes to make level and of equal size.

2. Beat together butter and shortening; blend in 4 cups powdered sugar, ½ cup milk and vanilla in large bowl. Beat with electric mixer until smooth. Add remaining 4 cups powdered sugar; beat until light and fluffy. Add more milk, 1 tablespoon at a time, as needed for good spreading consistency. Color ¾ cup frosting pastel blue and ¾ cup frosting pastel green; reserve 3 cups white frosting.

3. Cut cake board into 2 (7-inch) squares; stack. Cut remaining board into a 6½-inch square. Place 1 cake layer on 7-inch boards; frost top with ¾ cup white frosting. Top with second cake layer; frost top with ¾ cup white frosting.

4. Place 6½-inch board on top of cake. Top with third cake layer. Frost top with ¾ cup white frosting. Top with fourth cake layer.

5. Cover top and sides of cake with light coating of jelly to seal in crumbs. Frost opposite sides of cake with blue frosting. Frost other 2 sides with green frosting. Frost top of cake with ¾ cup white frosting.

6. Outline edges with chocolate pieces as shown in photo.

7. Using cookie cutter, make outline on top of block. Using writing tip and remaining white frosting, pipe outline of design. Fill with sprinkles and colored sugar.

8. Slice and serve top 2 layers of cake first. To serve bottom section, remove cake board; slice into pieces.

FUN TIP

Personalize cake by adding favorite colors and candies, spelling out child's name in candy or drawing special toy on top of cake.

Alphabet Block Cake

Baseball Fan Cake

This sporty design is so easy because the hat and bat are made from a cupcake and a cake roll-up.

Makes 16 servings

CAKES & FROSTINGS

- **2 (8-inch) square cakes**
- **1 recipe Creamy Decorator's Frosting (page 2)**
- **Paste food coloring in your team's colors**
- **Brown paste food coloring**
- **1 to 2 tablespoons milk**
- **1 recipe Creamy White Frosting (page 3)**
- **1 purchased cupcake**
- **1 small purchased cream-filled cake roll-up**

EQUIPMENT

- **1 (19×13-inch) cake board, covered**
- **4 decorating bags with couplers**
- **Tips: Numbers 2, 13 or 15, and 30 or 31**

1. Trim tops and sides of cakes.

2. To tint Creamy Decorator's Frosting, tint ¾ cup as desired for primary color of cap, ¼ cup as desired for secondary color of cap, ½ cup light brown and reserve 1 cup for white frosting. Thin remaining Creamy Decorator's Frosting with milk, adding 1 teaspoon at a time, until frosting is a thin consistency.

3. Place one cake on prepared cake board. Frost top with about ½ cup Creamy White Frosting. Place second cake on top. Frost top and sides with thinned frosting to seal in crumbs. Frost again with remaining Creamy White Frosting. Smooth frosting on top and sides.

4. For crown of baseball cap, place cupcake upside down on cake top, positioning about 1 inch from left edge of cake and aligning top edge of cupcake with cake center. Use toothpick to outline bill of cap in frosting.

5. Pipe tiny stars on cupcake and outlined bill with primary color of frosting and number 13 tip, as shown in photo 1.

6. Pipe letter on front of cap with secondary color of frosting and number 2 tip. Pipe large dot for button on top of cap with same frosting and tip.

7. To make bat, cut cake roll-up lengthwise in half. Place 1 piece on angle in upper right corner of cake with rounded side up.

8. Cut remaining piece crosswise in half. Trim sides of 1 half on an angle to resemble grip of bat and place at end of piece on cake, tapered end down. Cut a horizontal slice from bottom of remaining piece and place at tapered end of grip as shown in photo 2.

9. Pipe tiny stars all over bat with brown frosting and number 13 tip. Pipe message in desired writing with secondary color of frosting and number 2 tip.

10. Pipe bottom and top star borders with reserved white frosting and number 30 tip. Pipe small stars and dots as border accents with cap colors and number 13 and number 2 tips.

Baseball Fan Cake

1

2

Tugboat Cake

To create a river or lake for your tugboat, use blue plastic wrap to cover the cake board. If you like, crinkle extra plastic wrap and arrange it on board to resemble waves.

Makes 16 to 20 servings

CAKE & FROSTINGS

- **1 (13×9-inch) cake**
- **1 recipe Creamy White Frosting (page 3)**
- **Green, yellow and blue paste food coloring**
- **1 recipe Base Frosting (page 3)**

DECORATIONS & EQUIPMENT

- **2 (19×13-inch) cake boards**
- **Blue plastic wrap**
- **Green, yellow and blue sugar (optional)**
- **1 chocolate sugar wafer**
- **White or colored candy circles**
- **5 gummy candy circles**
- **Gummy fish (optional)**

1. Trim top and sides of cake. Cut cake as shown in diagram 1 with serrated knife, using ruler as guide.

2. Tint 2 cups Creamy White Frosting green, ¾ cup Creamy White Frosting yellow and ½ cup Creamy White Frosting blue.

3. Stack cake boards and cover with 2 layers of plastic wrap. Position one piece A in center of prepared cake board. Frost top with some of the green frosting. Top with second piece A. Frost top and sides with some of the Base Frosting to seal in crumbs. Frost again with remaining green frosting. Sprinkle top with green sugar, if desired.

4. Frost sides and top of piece B with some of the Base Frosting. Frost again with yellow frosting. Sprinkle with yellow sugar, if desired. Frost sides and top of piece C with Base Frosting. Frost again with blue frosting. Sprinkle with blue sugar, if desired.

5. Position yellow and blue pieces as shown in diagram 2.

6. Cut wafer in half crosswise. Press halves together; place on cake as shown in photo. Decorate with candies as shown.

Tugboat Cake

1

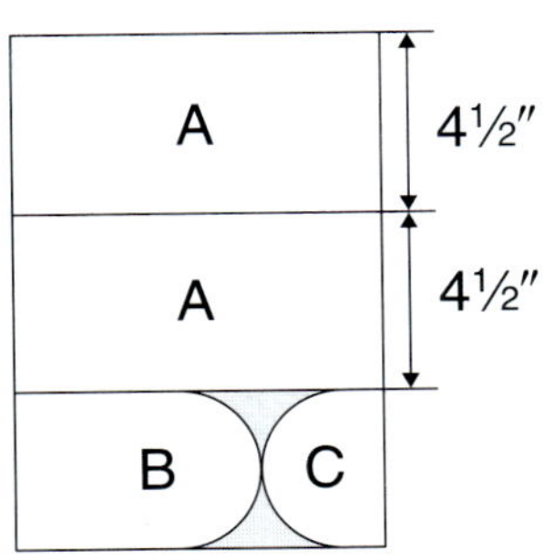

2

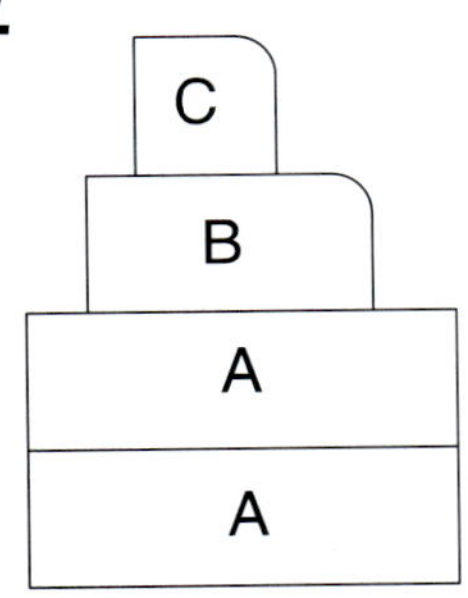

Treasure Chest

Makes 8 servings

1 package (12 ounces) pound cake
1 tub (8 ounces) COOL WHIP® Whipped Topping, thawed
Assorted candies for "jewels"
1 pretzel rod, cut into thirds
Black licorice
2 pretzels

CUT ½-inch slice off top of cake; set aside. Hollow out center of cake, leaving ½-inch shell on bottom and sides. Spoon 1 cup of the whipped topping into cake shell. Frost sides with 1½ cups whipped topping.

REFRIGERATE until ready to serve. Just before serving, place assorted "jewels" over whipped topping in cake shell. Angle reserved cake slice over jewels using pretzel rod pieces to resemble open chest lid. Frost slice with remaining whipped topping. Decorate cake with candies. Add pretzels for handles.

Birthday Extravaganza

Makes 12 to 14 servings

CAKES & FROSTING
2 (9-inch) round cake layers
1 recipe Creamy White Frosting (page 3)

DECORATIONS & EQUIPMENT
1 (10-inch) round cake board, covered
Assorted candies
Cookie Pops (page 65)
Rainbows (page 68)
1 decorating bag
Tip: Number 31

1. Trim tops of cakes. Place one cake layer on cake board. Frost top with about ½ cup Creamy White Frosting. Place second cake on top. Frost with Creamy White Frosting, reserving 1¼ cups for borders.

2. Sprinkle candies on cake top to resemble confetti. Place Cookie Pops and Rainbows on top of cake.

3. Place remaining 1¼ cups Creamy White Frosting in decorating bag fitted with number 31 tip. To pipe shell border, hold bag at 45° angle just above cake edge at top. Squeeze until small mound is formed for base of shell, lifting slightly. Continue squeezing while pulling tip away from base until desired length. Stop squeezing; lift tip. Position tip almost touching tail of first shell. Repeat technique, completing top and bottom borders. Place candies between shells on bottom border.

Note: For Cookie Pops, use teddy bear, candle, present and balloon cookie cutters. If not available, cut out squares for presents and circles for balloons.

Treasure Chest

Creative Cakes for the Holidays

Witch Cake

This scary cake will be the
hit at any child's Halloween party.

Makes 12 servings

INGREDIENTS

1 package (2-layer size) cake mix (any flavor), plus ingredients to prepare mix
2 containers (16 ounces each) cream cheese or vanilla frosting
Green food color
Black decorating gel
Black paste food color
Red string chewy fruit snacks
1 sugar ice cream cone
Assorted candies
Red fruit snack roll-up cutouts

SUPPLIES

1 (15×10-inch) cake board, covered, or large tray
Pastry bag and medium star tip
1 witch's black hat

1. Preheat oven to 350°F. Grease and flour 13×9-inch baking pan.

2. Prepare cake mix according to package directions; pour batter into prepared pan.

3. Bake 30 to 35 minutes or until wooden toothpick inserted into center comes out clean. Cool in pan on wire rack 10 minutes. Remove from pan to rack; cool completely.

4. Place cake on cake board. Spread top and sides of cake with 1 container frosting. Color half of remaining container of frosting with green food color.

5. Trace outline of head onto cake with toothpick. Fill in face with green frosting; outline with decorating gel.

6. Color remaining frosting with black paste food color. Spoon into pastry bag fitted with star tip; pipe frosting around edges of cake.

7. Cut hat in half lengthwise. Place one half on cake; discard remaining half. Place fruit snacks around hat to resemble hair. Decorate face as shown in photo.

Witch Cake

Macho Monster Cake

What fun to decorate a cake that is supposed to look ugly! Make your monster as scary as you can.

Makes 12 servings

INGREDIENTS

1 package (18.25 ounces) cake mix, any flavor, plus ingredients to prepare mix
1 container (16 ounces) cream cheese or vanilla frosting
Green and yellow food color
Black decorating gel
1 white chocolate baking bar (2 ounces)

SUPPLIES

1 (13×9-inch) cake board, covered, or large tray

1. Preheat oven to 350°F. Grease and flour 13×9-inch baking pan.

2. Prepare cake mix according to package directions. Pour into prepared pan.

3. Bake 30 to 35 minutes until wooden toothpick inserted into center comes out clean. Cool in pan on wire rack 10 minutes. Remove from pan to rack; cool completely.

4. Color frosting with green and yellow food color to make ugly monster green as shown in photo. Using diagram 1 as guide, cut pieces out (see Note).

5. Position pieces on prepared cake board as shown in diagram 2, connecting with some frosting. Frost cake. Using decorating gel, pipe eyes, mouth, hair and scars as shown. Break white chocolate baking bar into irregular pieces; position inside mouth as teeth.

Note: For cleaner cutting lines and fewer crumbs, place the cooled cake in the freezer for 30 to 45 minutes before cutting.

FUN TIP

Using the diagram as a guide, draw pattern pieces on waxed paper. Cut pieces out and place them on cake. Cut around pattern pieces with knife. Remove pattern pieces and discard.

Macho Monster Cake

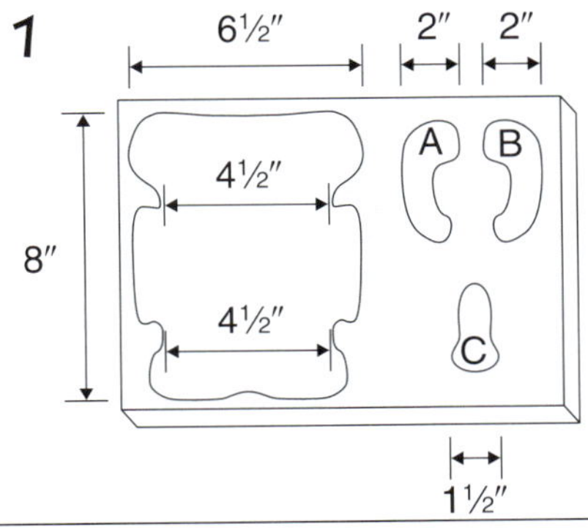

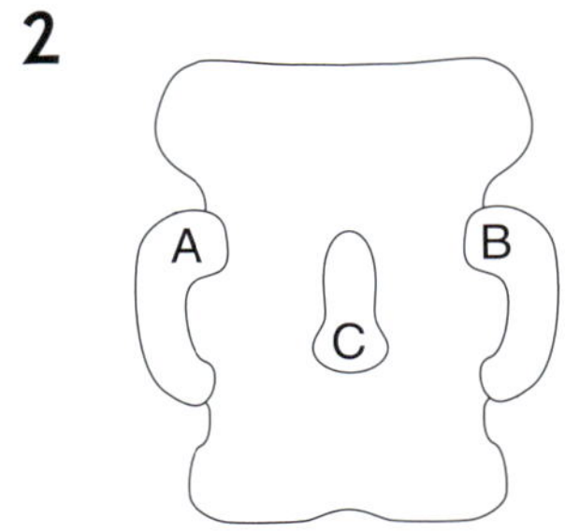

Turkey Cake

Don't expect to have leftovers from this turkey—it's sure to be gobbled up!

Makes 8 to 10 servings

CAKE & FROSTINGS

1 (8-inch) round cake layer
1 recipe Creamy White Frosting (page 3)
Red, orange and yellow paste food coloring
1 to 2 tablespoons milk
½ cup purchased chocolate frosting

DECORATIONS & EQUIPMENT

1 (19×13-inch) cake board, covered
¼ cup chopped walnuts
3 licorice sticks, cut 3 inches long
1 thin crosswise slice of licorice stick
1 red gummy worm, cut 3 inches long

1. Trim top of cake. Cut cake as shown in diagram 1 with serrated knife. Freeze pieces 30 to 45 minutes before frosting.

2. Tint ½ cup Creamy White Frosting deep red, ½ cup Creamy White Frosting deep orange and ½ cup Creamy White Frosting deep yellow. Thin remaining Creamy White Frosting with milk, adding 1 teaspoon at a time, until frosting is a thin consistency.

3. Hold 1 piece B in left hand. Starting at the point, carefully spread thinned frosting along the side, using long strokes in the direction away from point until all sides are frosted; frost top. Repeat with remaining pieces and thinned frosting to seal in crumbs.

4. Position piece A in center of prepared cake board as shown in photo. Frost sides and top with chocolate frosting. Sprinkle with walnuts.

5. Frost two B pieces with red frosting, two with orange frosting and two with yellow frosting as directed in step 3.

6. Position pieces around piece A as shown in diagram 2.

7. Position licorice and gummy worm as shown in photo.

FUN TIP

No chocolate frosting on hand? Just tint ½ cup Creamy White Frosting brown with brown paste food coloring.

Turkey Cake

1

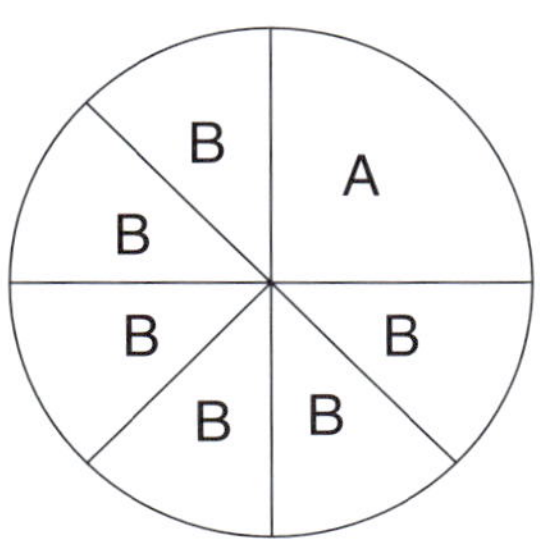

2

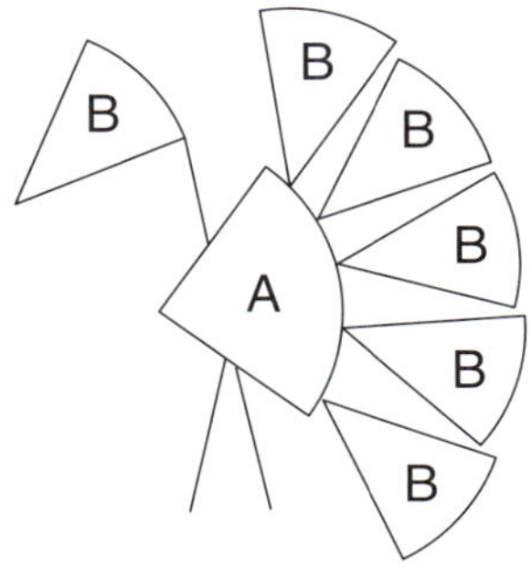

Dreidel Cake

This Hanukkah cake is sure to be a big hit—everyone's a winner with a spin of this dreidel!

Makes 12 servings

INGREDIENTS

- **1 package (2-layer size) cake mix, any flavor**
- **1¼ cups water**
- **3 eggs**
- **¾ cup sliced or slivered almonds, toasted and finely ground***
- **¼ cup vegetable oil**
- **½ teaspoon almond extract**
- **1½ containers (16 ounces each) cream cheese frosting**
- **Yellow and blue food colors**

SUPPLIES

- **1 large tray or (15×10-inch) cake board, covered**
- **Pastry bag and medium star tip**

**To toast almonds, place in single layer on baking sheet. Bake at 350°F for 7 to 10 minutes or until golden brown, stirring occasionally. Cool completely.*

1. Preheat oven to 350°F. Grease and flour 13×9-inch baking pan.

2. Combine cake mix, water, eggs, almonds, oil and extract in medium bowl. Beat at low speed of electric mixer until blended. Beat at medium speed 2 minutes. Pour batter into prepared pan.

3. Bake 35 to 40 minutes until wooden toothpick inserted into center comes out clean. Cool in pan on wire rack 10 minutes. Remove from pan; cool completely on rack.

4. Cut cake as shown in diagram 1. Position cake pieces on tray as shown in diagram 2, connecting pieces with small amount of frosting. Frost center of cake with about ½ cup white frosting as shown in photo.

5. Color about ¾ cup frosting yellow; spread onto top and sides of cake as shown in photo.

6. Using diagram 3 as guide, cut out letter; position on cake as shown in photo. Trace around pattern with wooden toothpick; remove pattern. Color remaining frosting blue. Spoon frosting into pastry bag fitted with star tip. Use to fill in letter and pipe around top edge of cake as shown in photo.

Dreidel Cake

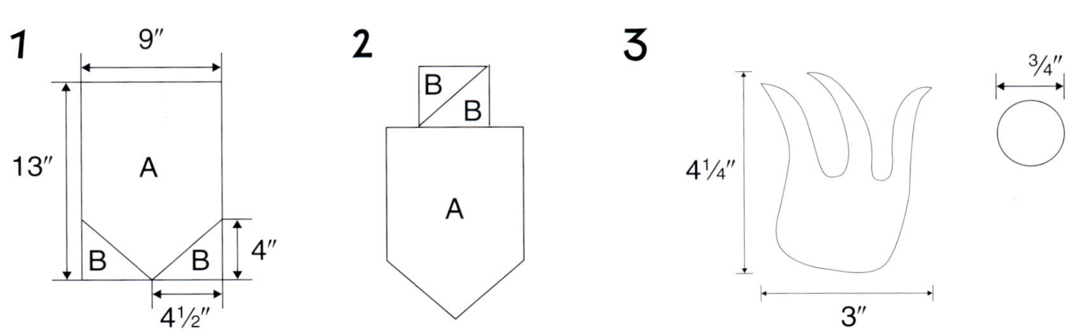

Chilly Snowman Cake

Make the spirit of winter last for months with this frosty snowman cake.

Makes 12 servings

INGREDIENTS

1 package (2-layer size) yellow cake mix, plus ingredients to prepare mix
1 cup butter brickle bits
22 round peppermint candies
1 recipe Cookie Glaze (recipe follows)
Confectioners' sugar
4 frosted mini shredded wheat cereal pieces
1 pretzel rod
1 recipe Fluffy White Frosting (page 2)
Coarse sugar (optional)*
6 to 8 large marshmallows, divided
Chewy fruit snack roll
Red string licorice
Assorted candies

SUPPLIES

1 large tray or (18×10-inch) cake board, covered

**Coarse sugar, sometimes called "pretzel sugar," can be found in specialty food stores. Although not necessary for the success of the recipe, it helps add a frosty look to the snowman.*

1. Preheat oven to 350°F. Grease and flour one 8-inch round baking pan and one 9-inch round baking pan; set aside.

2. Prepare cake mix according to package directions. Stir in butter brickle bits. Divide batter between prepared pans.

3. Bake 30 to 35 minutes or until wooden toothpick inserted into centers comes out clean. Cool in pans on wire racks 10 minutes. Remove from pans; cool completely on racks.

4. While cakes are cooling, cover baking sheet with foil. Arrange peppermints on prepared sheet to resemble hat as shown in photo. Bake at 350°F 4 to 5 minutes or until mints just begin to melt and stick together. Cool completely.

5. Prepare Cookie Glaze. Stir in enough additional confectioners' sugar to thicken slightly. Using thickened glaze, assemble snowman's broom by "gluing" together shredded wheat pieces and pretzel rod as shown in photo. Let stand until hardened.

6. Arrange cake rounds on tray with smaller round at top of tray. Frost entire cake with Fluffy White Frosting. Sprinkle with coarse sugar, if desired.

7. Place peppermint hat on top of snowman's head. Place 2 marshmallows under hat to support hat on tray, if necessary. Add broom and decorate rest of snowman as shown in photo.

Cookie Glaze

1 cup confectioners' sugar
1 to 1½ tablespoons milk

1. Combine sugar and enough milk to make a medium-thick pourable glaze.

Makes about 1 cup

Chilly Snowman Cake

Candy Cane Cake

Makes 12 to 16 servings

1 package DUNCAN HINES® Moist Deluxe Cake Mix (any flavor)

DECORATOR FROSTING

5 cups confectioners' sugar
¾ cup shortening
½ cup water
⅓ cup non-dairy powdered creamer
2 teaspoons vanilla extract
½ teaspoon salt
Red food coloring
Maraschino cherry halves, well drained

1. Preheat oven to 350°F. Grease and flour 13×9×2-inch pan.

2. Prepare, bake and cool cake following package directions for basic recipe. Remove from pan. Freeze cake for ease in handling.

3. For decorator frosting, combine confectioners sugar, shortening, water, non-dairy powdered creamer, vanilla extract and salt in large bowl. Beat at medium speed with electric mixer for 3 minutes. Beat at high speed for 5 minutes. Add more confectioners sugar to thicken or water to thin frosting as needed. Reserve 2 cups frosting. Tint remaining frosting with red food coloring.

4. Cut frozen cake and arrange as shown in diagrams 1 and 2. Spread white frosting on cake. Mark candy cane stripes in frosting with tip of knife. Place star tip in decorating bag and fill with red frosting. To make stripes, arrange maraschino cherry halves and pipe red frosting following lines.

FUN TIP

For a quick dessert, serve leftover cake pieces with sugared strawberries and dollops of whipped cream.

Candy Cane Cake

1

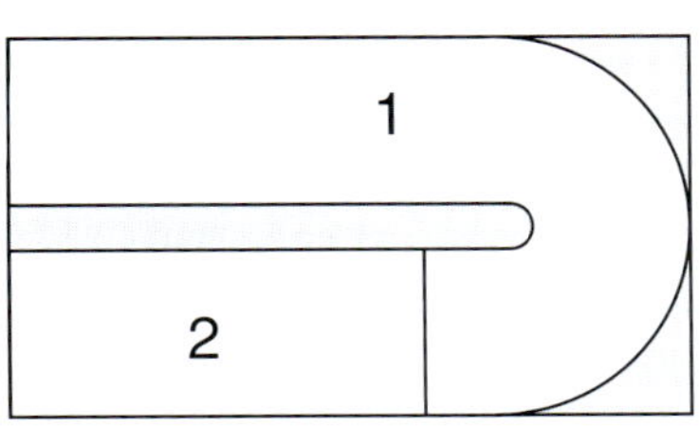

2

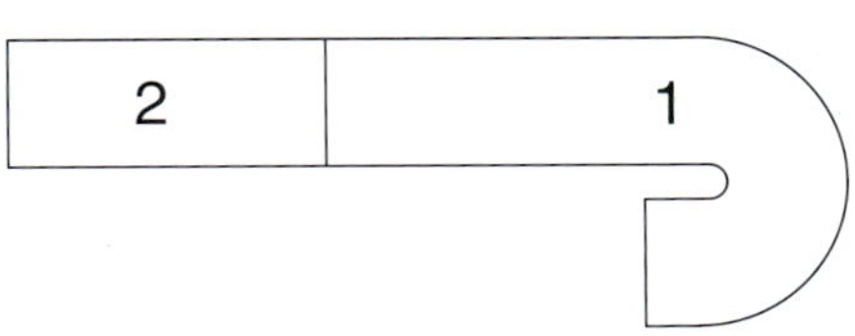

Angel Cake

This sweet angel is sure to disappear quickly.

Makes 8 to 10 servings

- **1 (8-inch) round cake layer**
- **1 recipe Creamy White Frosting (page 3)**
- **1 to 2 tablespoons milk**
- **5 tablespoons flaked coconut, divided**
- **Red liquid food coloring**
- **1 teaspoon water**
- **2 small blue jelly beans**
- **Silver edible glitter**

Cut cake as shown in diagram 1. Position cake pieces as shown in diagram 2, connecting with frosting. Thin 1½ cups frosting with milk, adding 1 teaspoon at a time, until frosting is of thin consistency. Frost entire cake with thinned frosting to seal in crumbs. Frost with remaining Creamy White Frosting.

Place 4 tablespoons coconut in resealable plastic food storage bag. Combine small amount of food coloring with water; add to bag. Shake until evenly coated. Toast remaining 1 tablespoon coconut in preheated 350°F oven about 5 minutes or until lightly browned. Sprinkle pink coconut on angel's body and toasted coconut on angel's head for hair. Place jelly beans on face for eyes. Sprinkle glitter over angel's wings.

Pretty Pink Heart

Makes 12 to 16 servings

- **1 package cake mix (2-layer size), any flavor except angel food**
- **1 cup cold milk**
- **1 package (4-serving size) JELL-O® Vanilla Flavor Instant Pudding & Pie Filling**
- **¼ cup powdered sugar**
- **1 tub (8 ounces) COOL WHIP® Whipped Topping, thawed**
- **¼ teaspoon red food coloring**
- **Multicolored sprinkles**

HEAT oven to 350°F.

PREPARE cake mix as directed on package. Divide batter evenly between greased and floured 8-inch round and 8-inch square baking pans. Bake as directed on package. Cool 10 minutes; remove from pans. Cool completely on wire racks.

POUR milk into medium bowl. Add pudding mix and sugar. Beat with wire whisk 2 minutes. Gently stir in whipped topping and food coloring.

CUT round cake in half. Place cut sides of round cake along two touching sides of square cake, using pudding mixture to hold pieces together. Frost cake with remaining pudding mixture. Decorate with sprinkles.

Angel Cake

1

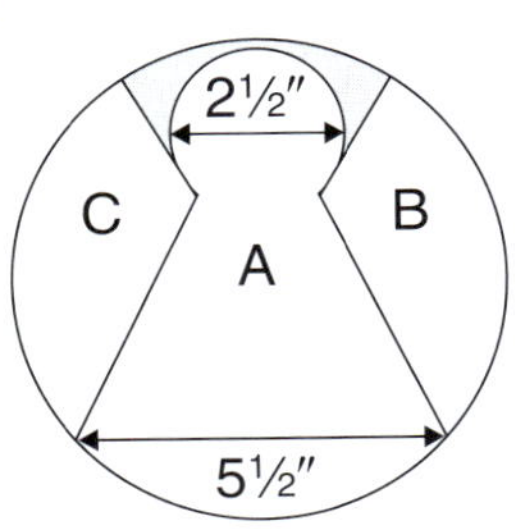

2

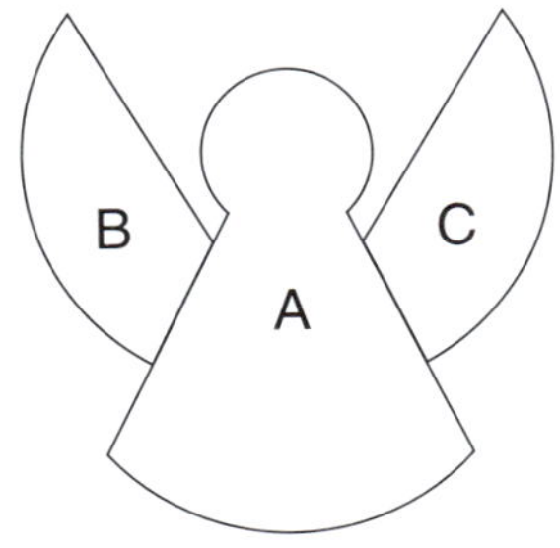

Hippity Hop Bunny Cake

Surprise the kids after the Easter egg hunt with this cake.

Makes 12 to 16 servings

$2\frac{1}{4}$ cups BAKER'S® ANGEL FLAKE® Coconut
Red food coloring
2 baked 9-inch round cake layers, cooled
1 tub (8 ounces) COOL WHIP® Whipped Topping, thawed
Assorted candies

TINT ¼ cup coconut pink using red food coloring.

LEAVE 1 cake layer whole; cut remaining cake layer as shown in diagram 2. Using small amount of whipped topping to hold pieces together, arrange cake on serving tray as shown in photograph.

FROST cake with remaining whipped topping. Sprinkle center of bunny's ears with pink coconut. Sprinkle remaining 2 cups white coconut over bunny's head and outer edges of ears. Decorate with candies. Store cake in refrigerator.

Lucky Shamrock

Makes 12 to 16 servings

$2\frac{2}{3}$ cups BAKER'S® ANGEL FLAKE® Coconut
Green food coloring
3 baked 9-inch round cake layers, cooled
$1\frac{2}{3}$ cups Vanilla Buttercream Frosting (recipe follows)
Green decorating icing

TINT coconut with green food coloring.

LEAVE 1 cake layer whole; cut 1-inch slice from remaining 2 cakes so that cake fits along curve of whole cake.

PREPARE Vanilla Buttercream Frosting. Using small amount of frosting to hold pieces together, arrange whole cake at top of serving tray. Place other 2 cakes along lower edges of whole cake, fitting cut ends along curve. Place 2 small slices between 2 layers as stem.

FROST cake with remaining frosting. Sprinkle with coconut. Using decorating icing, outline the cake.

Vanilla Buttercream Frosting

1 package (16 ounces) powdered sugar (about 4 cups)
½ cup (1 stick) margarine or butter, softened
3 tablespoons milk
2 teaspoons vanilla

BEAT sugar, margarine, milk and vanilla with electric mixer on low speed until smooth. If frosting becomes too thick, beat in additional milk by teaspoonfuls until of spreading consistency.

Makes about $2\frac{1}{2}$ cups

Hippity Hop Bunny Cake

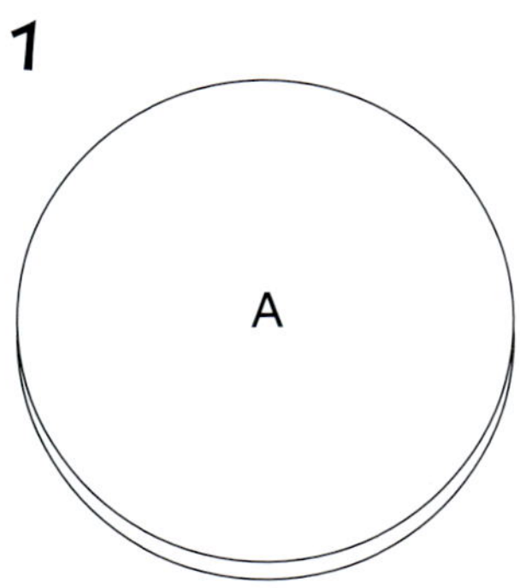

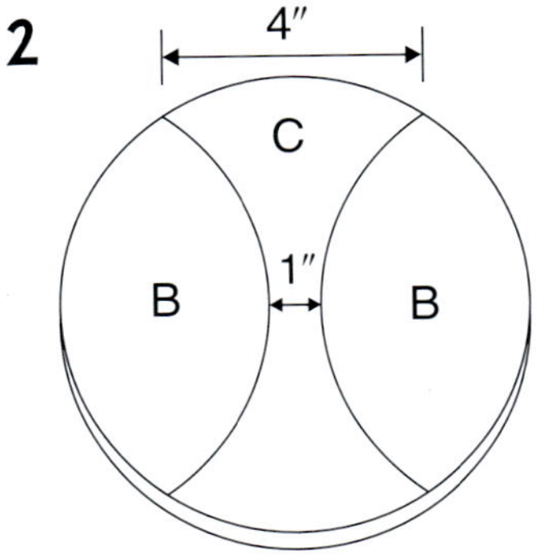

Liberty Bell Cake

Start your 4th of July festivities off with a bang by serving this all-American cake.

Makes 16 servings

CAKE & FROSTINGS

1 (13×9-inch) cake
1 recipe Creamy White Frosting (page 3)
1 recipe Base Frosting (page 3)
Blue decorating gel

DECORATIONS & EQUIPMENT

1 (19×13-inch) cake board, covered
1 (1½-inch) star cookie cutter
Red cinnamon candies

1. Trim top and sides of cake. Cut cake as shown in diagram 1.

2. Position pieces on prepared cake board as shown in diagram 2, connecting with some of the Creamy White Frosting.

3. Frost entire cake with Base Frosting. Frost again with remaining Creamy White Frosting.

4. Gently press cookie cutter into frosting on bell, leaving imprints. Trace outline of imprint with gel. Evenly fill in each star with gel.

5. Decorate with candies as shown in photo.

Flag Dessert

This patriotic dessert is ideal to let the kids decorate!

Makes 15 servings

2 pints fresh strawberries
1 package (12 ounces) pound cake, cut into 16 slices
1⅓ cups blueberries
1 tub (12 ounces) COOL WHIP® Whipped Topping, thawed

SLICE 1 cup strawberries; set aside. Halve remaining strawberries; set aside.

LINE bottom of 12×8-inch glass baking dish with 8 cake slices. Top with 1 cup sliced strawberries, 1 cup blueberries and ½ whipped topping. Place remaining cake slices over whipped topping. Spread remaining whipped topping over cake. Arrange strawberry halves and remaining ⅓ cup blueberries over whipped topping to create a flag design.

REFRIGERATE until ready to serve.

Liberty Bell Cake

1

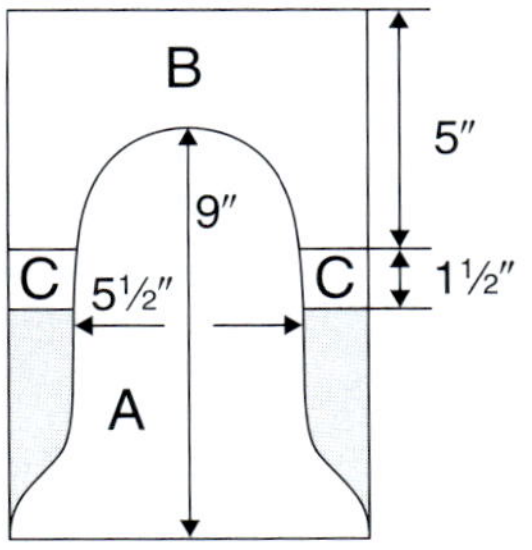

2

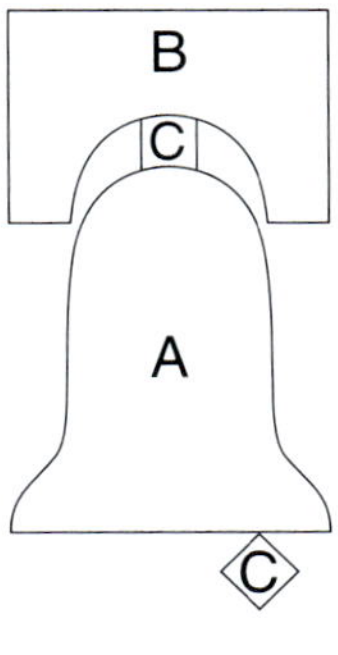

Sweet Treats for Festive Occasions

Pumpkin Candy Brownies

Makes 26 brownies

1 package DUNCAN HINES® Chocolate Lovers Double Fudge Brownie Mix
2 eggs
⅓ cup water
¼ cup vegetable Oil
1 cup DUNCAN HINES® Chocolate Frosting
26 pumpkin candies
½ cup DUNCAN HINES® Vanilla Frosting
Green food coloring

1. Preheat oven to 350°F. Line 26 (2-inch) muffin cups with foil liners or place on baking sheets.

2. Combine brownie mix, contents of fudge packet from mix, eggs, water and oil in large bowl. Stir with spoon until well blended, about 50 strokes. Fill each foil liner with 2 level measuring tablespoons batter. Bake 15 to 17 minutes or until firm. Cool 5 to 10 minutes in pans. Remove to cooling racks.

3. Place Chocolate frosting in small saucepan. Melt on low heat, stirring constantly. Frost top of 1 warm brownie with generous ½ teaspoonful melted frosting. Top with 1 pumpkin candy; push down slightly. Repeat for remaining brownies. Cool completely.

4. Tint Vanilla frosting with green food coloring. Place in decorating bag fitted with small leaf tip. Pipe 3 leaves around each pumpkin candy. Use small writing tip to pipe vines, if desired.

Pumpkin Candy Brownies

Halloween Cookie Pizza

Makes about 16 to 20 servings

¾ cup packed light brown sugar
½ cup butter flavor shortening
1 egg
1 tablespoon water
1 teaspoon vanilla extract
1¼ cups all-purpose flour
½ teaspoon baking soda
¼ teaspoon salt
1 cup REESE'S® Peanut Butter Chips
1 cup miniature marshmallows
½ cup HERSHEY®'S Semi-Sweet Chocolate Chips
½ cup chopped pecans
Chocolate Drizzle (recipe follows)
Orange Drizzle (recipe follows)

1. Heat oven to 350°F. Lightly grease 12-inch round pizza pan.

2. In large bowl, beat brown sugar and shortening until creamy. Add egg, water and vanilla; beat well. Stir together flour, baking soda and salt; add to sugar mixture, beating on low speed of electric mixer until well blended. Stir in peanut butter chips. Spread batter into prepared pan to within ½ inch of edge.

3. Bake 11 to 13 minutes or until set. Remove from oven. Sprinkle marshmallows, chocolate chips and pecans over top. Return to oven. Bake 5 to 7 minutes or until marshmallows are lightly browned. Cool completely.

4. Prepare Chocolate Drizzle and Orange Drizzle. Drizzle Chocolate Drizzle over top. Drizzle Orange Drizzle over chocolate. Let stand about 1 hour until drizzles set. Cut into wedges.

Chocolate Drizzle: In small microwave-safe bowl, place ¼ cup HERSHEY®'S Semi-Sweet Chocolate Chips and 1½ teaspoons butter flavor shortening. Microwave at MEDIUM (50%) 1 minute; stir. If necessary, microwave at MEDIUM an additional 15 seconds at a time, stirring after each heating, just until chips are melted when stirred.

Orange Drizzle: In small bowl, stir together ½ cup powdered sugar, 1 tablespoon water, 3 drops yellow food color and 2 drops red food color; stir until well blended.

Turkey Cupcakes

Cupcakes are always a welcome treat for kids. These are sure to command a repeat performance!

Makes 2 dozen cupcakes

INGREDIENTS

1 package (2-layer size) cake mix (any flavor), plus ingredients to prepare mix
1 container (16 ounces) chocolate frosting
¾ cup marshmallow creme
24 shortbread ring cookies
48 small red candies
Decorations: candy corn, assorted candies

SUPPLIES

24 regular-size (2½-inch) paper muffin cup liners

1. Preheat oven to 350°F. Line 24 muffin cups with paper muffin cup liners.

2. Prepare cake mix according to package directions. Spoon batter into prepared muffin pans.

3. Bake 15 to 20 minutes or until wooden toothpick inserted into centers comes out clean. Cool in pans on wire racks 10 minutes. Remove to racks; cool completely.

4. Combine frosting and marshmallow creme in medium bowl; mix well. Frost cupcakes lightly with frosting mixture; reserve remaining frosting mixture.

5. Cut cookies in half. Cut half of them in half again to form quarters.

6. For each cupcake, place larger cookie piece cut-side down on back edge of cupcake for tail. Place 1 of the 2 smaller cookie pieces cut-side down on opposite side of cupcake for head; discard remaining smaller cookie piece or reserve for another use. Frost cookies with remaining frosting mixture so they blend in with cupcake.

7. Position candies on heads for eyes. Decorate tops of tails with candies as desired.

Jolly Peanut Butter Gingerbread Cookies

Makes about 6 dozen cookies

1⅔ cups (10-ounce package) REESE'S® Peanut Butter Chips
¾ cup (1½ sticks) butter or margarine, softened
1 cup packed light brown sugar
1 cup dark corn syrup
2 eggs
5 cups all-purpose flour
1 teaspoon baking soda
½ teaspoon ground cinnamon
¼ teaspoon ground ginger
¼ teaspoon salt

1. In small microwave-safe bowl, place peanut butter chips. Microwave at HIGH (100%) 1 to 2 minutes or until chips are melted when stirred. In large bowl, beat melted peanut butter chips and butter until well blended. Add brown sugar, corn syrup and eggs; beat until light and fluffy. Stir together flour, baking soda, cinnamon, ginger and salt. Add half of flour mixture to butter mixture; beat on low speed of electric mixer until smooth. With wooden spoon, stir in remaining flour mixture until well blended. Divide into thirds; wrap each in plastic wrap. Refrigerate 1 hour or until dough is firm enough to roll.

2. Heat oven to 325°F.

3. On lightly floured surface, roll 1 dough portion at a time to ⅛-inch thickness; with floured cookie cutters, cut into holiday shapes. Place on ungreased cookie sheet.

4. Bake 10 to 12 minutes or until set and lightly browned. Cool slightly; remove from cookie sheet to wire rack. Cool completely. Frost and decorate as desired.

Jolly Peanut Butter Gingerbread Cookies

Conversation Heart Cereal Treats

Makes 12 bars

2 tablespoons margarine or butter
20 large marshmallows
3 cups frosted oat cereal with marshmallow bits
12 large conversation hearts

1. Line 8- or 9-inch square pan with aluminum foil, leaving 2-inch overhangs on 2 sides. Generously grease or spray with nonstick cooking spray.

2. Melt margarine and marshmallows over medium heat 3 minutes or until melted and smooth; stir constantly. Remove from heat.

3. Add cereal; stir until completely coated. Scrape into prepared pan and press evenly onto bottom using greased rubber spatula. Press candies into top of treats while still warm, evenly spacing to allow 1 candy per bar. Let cool 10 minutes. Using foil overhangs as handles, remove treats from pan. Cut into 12 bars.

Valentine's Day Cookie Cards

Create your own Valentine's Day message for that special valentine.

Makes 1 dozen cookies

INGREDIENTS
1 recipe Butter Cookie Dough (page 5)
1 container (16 ounces) vanilla frosting
1 container (16 ounces) pink cherry-flavored frosting
Assorted candies

SUPPLIES
Pastry bags and assorted decorating tips

1. Preheat oven to 350°F. Grease cookie sheets.

2. On lightly floured surface, roll out cookie dough to ⅛-inch thickness. Cut out 4½×3-inch rectangular cookies or use heart-shaped cookie cutter. Place on prepared cookie sheets.

3. Bake 8 to 10 minutes or until edges are lightly browned. Remove to wire racks; cool completely.

4. Spread cookies with desired frostings; spoon remaining frostings into pastry bags fitted with decorating tips. Decorate cookies with frostings and candies to resemble Valentine's Day cards.

Conversation Heart Cereal Treats

Shamrock Ice Cream Sandwiches

Use other holiday-shaped cookie cutters and color the dough the appropriate color.

Makes 6 to 8 cookie sandwiches

INGREDIENTS

1 recipe Butter Cookie Dough (page 5)
3 or 4 drops green food color
1 pint softened ice cream or frozen yogurt, any flavor

SUPPLIES

3½- to 5-inch shamrock-shaped cookie cutter

1. Prepare cookie dough; mix in food color. Cover; refrigerate until firm, about 4 hours or overnight.

2. Preheat oven to 350°F.

3. Roll dough on floured surface to ¼-inch thickness. Cut out cookies using cookie cutter. Place on ungreased cookie sheets.

4. Bake 8 to 10 minutes or until cookies are lightly browned around edges. Remove cookies to wire racks; cool completely.

5. Remove ice cream from freezer; let stand at room temperature to soften slightly, about 10 minutes. Spread 4 to 5 tablespoons ice cream onto flat sides of half of the cookies. Place remaining cookies, flat sides down, on ice cream; press cookies together lightly.

6. Wrap each sandwich in foil; freeze until firm, about 2 hours or overnight.

St. Patrick's Parfaits

They'll all be wearing the green with this fun-to-make, fun-to-eat dessert.

Makes 4 servings

2 cups cold milk
1 package (4-serving size) JELL-O® Pistachio Flavor Instant Pudding and Pie Filling
Chocolate sauce
2 cups thawed COOL WHIP® Whipped Topping
Chocolate shamrock cutouts (optional)

POUR milk into large bowl. Add pudding mix. Beat with wire whisk 1 to 2 minutes.

LAYER pudding, chocolate sauce and 1 cup whipped topping alternately in 4 parfait glasses. Garnish with remaining whipped topping and chocolate shamrock cutouts. Refrigerate until ready to serve.

Shamrock Ice Cream Sandwiches

Frosted Easter Cut-Outs

Makes about 3½ dozen cookies

COOKIES

1¼ cups granulated sugar
1 Butter Flavor* CRISCO® Stick or 1 cup Butter Flavor CRISCO® all-vegetable shortening
2 eggs
¼ cup light corn syrup or regular pancake syrup
1 tablespoon vanilla
3 cups all-purpose flour plus 4 tablespoons, divided
¾ teaspoon baking powder
½ teaspoon baking soda
½ teaspoon salt

ICING

1 cup confectioners' sugar
2 tablespoons milk
Food color (optional)
Decorating icing

**Butter Flavor Crisco is artificially flavored.*

1. Place granulated sugar and shortening in large bowl. Beat at medium speed of electric mixer until well blended. Add eggs, syrup and vanilla; beat until well blended and fluffy.

2. Combine 3 cups flour, baking powder, baking soda and salt. Add gradually to shortening mixture, beating at low speed until well blended.

3. Divide dough into 4 equal pieces; shape each into disk. Wrap with plastic wrap. Refrigerate 1 hour or until firm.

4. Heat oven to 375°F. Place sheets of foil on countertop for cooling cookies.

5. Sprinkle about 1 tablespoon flour on large sheet of waxed paper. Place disk of dough on floured paper; flatten slightly with hands. Turn dough over; cover with another large sheet of waxed paper. Roll dough to ¼-inch thickness. Remove top sheet of waxed paper. Cut into desired shapes with floured cookie cutter. Place 2 inches apart on ungreased baking sheet. Repeat with remaining dough.

6. Bake one baking sheet at a time at 375°F for 5 to 7 minutes or until edges of cookies are lightly browned. *Do not overbake.* Cool 2 minutes on baking sheet. Remove cookies to foil to cool completely.

7. For icing, combine confectioners' sugar and milk; stir until smooth. Add food color, if desired. Stir until blended. Spread icing on cookies; place on foil until icing is set. Decorate as desired with decorating icing.

Frosted Easter Cut-Outs

Color-Bright Ice Cream Sandwiches

Makes about 24 ice cream sandwiches

- **¾ cup (1½ sticks) butter or margarine, softened**
- **¾ cup creamy peanut butter**
- **1¼ cups firmly packed light brown sugar**
- **1 large egg**
- **1 teaspoon vanilla extract**
- **1½ cups all-purpose flour**
- **1 teaspoon baking soda**
- **¼ teaspoon salt**
- **1¾ cups "M&M's"® Chocolate Mini Baking Bits, divided**
- **2 quarts vanilla or chocolate ice cream, slightly softened**

Preheat oven to 350°F. In large bowl cream butter, peanut butter and sugar until light and fluffy; beat in egg and vanilla. In medium bowl combine flour, baking soda and salt; blend into creamed mixture. Stir in 1⅓ cups "M&M's"® Chocolate Mini Baking Bits. Shape dough into 1¼-inch balls. Place about 2 inches apart on ungreased cookie sheets. Gently flatten to about ½-inch thickness with fingertips. Place 7 or 8 of the remaining "M&M's"® Chocolate Mini Baking Bits on each cookie; press in lightly. Bake 10 to 12 minutes or until edges are light brown. Do not overbake. Cool about 1 minute on cookie sheets; cool completely on wire racks. Assemble cookies in pairs with about ⅓ cup ice cream; press cookies together lightly. Wrap each sandwich in plastic wrap; freeze until firm.

Star Spangled Snack

Makes 8 servings

- **1 package (4-serving size) JELL-O® Brand Berry Blue Flavor Gelatin**
- **1 package (4-serving size) JELL-O® Brand Gelatin, any red flavor**
- **2 cups boiling water**
- **1 cup cold water**
- **1 tub (8 ounces) COOL WHIP® Whipped Topping, thawed**

DISSOLVE each package of gelatin completely in 1 cup boiling water in separate bowls. Stir ½ cup cold water into each bowl of gelatin. Pour each mixture into separate 8-inch square pans. Refrigerate at least 3 hours or until firm. Cut gelatin in each pan into ½-inch cubes.

SPOON blue cubes evenly into 8 dessert dishes. Cover with whipped topping. Top with red cubes. Garnish with remaining whipped topping.

REFRIGERATE until ready to serve.

Color-Bright Ice Cream Sandwiches

Cookies & More Just for Kids

Bunch O' Balloons

You could use sugar cookie dough instead of chocolate chip in this recipe if you wish. These fun cookies could also be decorated to be Halloween pumpkin cookies or holiday ornament cookies.

Makes 8 servings

1 package (20 ounces) refrigerated chocolate chip cookie dough
1 tub (8 ounces) COOL WHIP® Whipped Topping, thawed
Assorted fruits and candies
Decorating gel
Red string licorice

HEAT oven to 350°F.

SLICE cookie dough evenly into 8 slices. Pat each slice into 5-inch circle on lightly floured surface. Place 2 inches apart on ungreased cookie sheets.

BAKE 10 to 12 minutes or until lightly browned. Remove from cookie sheets. Cool completely on wire racks.

SPREAD whipped topping evenly onto each cookie. Decorate with fruit, candy and gel. Arrange decorated cookies on large serving tray to resemble a bunch of balloons. Place a piece of licorice at bottom edge on each cookie to resemble string. Tie strings together with additional licorice. Serve immediately.

Bunch O' Balloons

Cookie Cups

Makes 12 cookie cups

1 package (20 ounces) refrigerated sugar cookie dough
All-purpose flour (optional)
Prepared pudding, nondairy whipped topping, maraschino cherries, jelly beans, assorted sprinkles and small candies

1. Grease 12 (2¾-inch) muffin cups.

2. Remove dough from wrapper according to package directions. Sprinkle dough with flour to minimize sticking, if necessary.

3. Cut dough into 12 equal pieces; roll into balls. Place 1 ball in bottom of each muffin cup. Press dough halfway up sides of muffin cup, making indentation in center of dough.

4. Freeze muffin cups 15 minutes. Preheat oven to 350°F. Bake 15 to 17 minutes or until golden brown. Cookies will be puffy. Remove from oven; gently press indentation with teaspoon.

5. Return to oven 1 to 2 minutes. Cool cookies in muffin cups 5 minutes. Remove to wire racks; cool completely.

6. Fill each cookie cup with desired fillings. Decorate as desired.

Giant Cookie Cups Variation: Grease 10 (3¾-inch) muffin cups. Cut dough into 10 pieces; roll into balls. Complete recipe according to regular Cookie Cup directions.

Makes 10 giant cookie cups

FUN TIP

Add some pizzazz to your cookie cups by filling with a mixture of prepared fruit-flavored gelatin combined with prepared pudding or nondairy whipped topping.

Frozen Fudge Pops

Makes 6 to 8 fudge pops

2 cups milk
⅓ cup honey*
3 tablespoons unsweetened cocoa powder
2 tablespoons cornstarch
1 teaspoon vanilla
1 teaspoon butter or margarine

**Honey should not be fed to infants under one year of age. Honey is a safe and wholesome food for older children.*

Combine milk, honey, cocoa, cornstarch, vanilla and butter in medium saucepan. Cook and stir over low heat until little bubbles appear and mixture thickens. Remove from heat; cool slightly and pour into popsicle molds. Freeze 2 to 4 hours or until firm. Store in freezer.

Favorite recipe from **National Honey Board**

Cookie Cups

Dirt Cups

This kid-pleasing favorite can also be made in a clean, new flower pot and decorated with lollipop "flowers."

Makes 8 to 10 servings

1 package (16 ounces) chocolate sandwich cookies
2 cups cold milk
1 package (4-serving size) JELL-O® Chocolate Flavor Instant Pudding & Pie Filling
1 tub (8 ounces) COOL WHIP® Whipped Topping, thawed
8 to 10 (7-ounce) paper or plastic cups
Suggested garnishes: gummy worms or other gummy candies, candy flowers, chopped peanuts, granola

Crush cookies in zipper-style plastic food storage bag with rolling pin or in food processor.

Pour cold milk into large bowl. Add pudding mix. Beat with wire whisk 2 minutes. Let stand 5 minutes or until thickened. Stir in whipped topping and ½ of crushed cookies.

Place about 1 tablespoon crushed cookies into each cup. Fill cups about ¾ full with pudding mixture. Top with remaining crushed cookies.

Refrigerate until ready to serve. Garnish just before serving.

Sand Cups: Use one package (12 ounces) vanilla wafer cookies and JELL-O® Vanilla Flavor Instant Pudding & Pie Filling.

Chocolate Peanut Butter Cups

Makes 30 servings

1 package DUNCAN HINES® Moist Deluxe Swiss Chocolate Cake Mix
1 container DUNCAN HINES® Vanilla Frosting
½ cup peanut butter
15 miniature peanut butter cup candies, wrappers removed, cut in half vertically

1. Preheat oven to 350°F. Place 30 (2½-inch) paper liners in muffin cups.

2. Prepare, bake and cool cupcakes following package directions for basic recipe.

3. Combine Vanilla frosting and peanut butter in medium bowl. Stir until smooth. Frost one cupcake. Decorate with peanut butter cup candy, cut-side down. Repeat with remaining cupcakes.

Peanut Butter Jumbos

Makes about 1½ dozen cookies

½ cup butter or margarine, softened
1 cup packed brown sugar
1 cup granulated sugar
1½ cups peanut butter
3 eggs
2 teaspoons baking soda
1 teaspoon vanilla
4½ cups uncooked rolled oats
1 cup (6 ounces) semisweet chocolate chips
1 cup candy-coated chocolate pieces

Preheat oven to 350°F. Lightly grease cookie sheets.

Beat butter, sugars, peanut butter and eggs in large bowl until well blended. Blend in baking soda, vanilla and oats until well mixed. Stir in chocolate chips and candy pieces.

Scoop out about ⅓ cupful of dough for each cookie. Place on prepared cookie sheets, spacing about 4 inches apart. Press each cookie to flatten slightly. Bake 15 to 20 minutes or until firm in center. Remove to wire racks to cool.

Peanut Butter Jumbo Sandwiches: Prepare cookies as directed. Place ⅓ cup softened chocolate or vanilla ice cream on cookie bottom. Top with cookie. Lightly press sandwich together. Repeat with remaining cookies. Wrap sandwiches in plastic wrap; freeze until firm.

Cookie Pops

Makes 20 cookies

1 package (20 ounces) refrigerated sugar cookie dough
All-purpose flour (optional)
20 (4-inch) lollipop sticks
Assorted colored sugars, frostings, glazes and gels

1. Preheat oven to 350°F. Grease cookie sheets.

2. Remove dough from wrapper according to package directions.

3. Sprinkle with flour to minimize sticking, if necessary. Cut dough in half. Reserve 1 half; refrigerate remaining dough.

4. Roll reserved dough to ⅛-inch thickness. Cut out cookies using 3½-inch cookie cutters.

5. Place lollipop sticks on cookies so that tips of sticks are imbedded in cookies. Carefully turn cookies so sticks are in back; place on prepared cookie sheets. Repeat with remaining dough.

6. Bake 7 to 11 minutes or until edges are lightly browned. Cool cookies on cookie sheets 2 minutes. Remove cookies to wire racks; cool completely.

7. Decorate with colored sugars, frostings, glazes and gels as desired.

Purple Cow Jumped Over the Moon

Milk shakes are all-time favorites with kids. Any one of these fruity low-fat shakes is sure to win raves.

Makes 8 (½-cup) servings

- **3 cups vanilla nonfat frozen yogurt**
- **1 cup milk**
- **½ cup thawed frozen grape juice concentrate (undiluted)**
- **1½ teaspoons lemon juice**

1. Place yogurt, milk, grape juice concentrate and lemon juice in food processor or blender container; process until smooth. Serve immediately.

Chocolate Rootbeer Shake: Place 1 quart vanilla nonfat frozen yogurt, 1 cup vanilla nonfat yogurt and ¼ cup chocolate nonfat syrup in food processor or blender container; process until smooth. Pour ½ of mixture evenly into 12 glasses; top with ½ of (12-ounce) can root beer. Fill glasses equally with remaining yogurt mixture; top with remaining root beer.

Makes 12 (⅔-cup) servings

Sunshine Shake: Place 1 quart vanilla nonfat frozen yogurt, 1⅓ cups orange juice, 1 cup fresh or thawed frozen raspberries and 1 teaspoon sugar in food processor or blender container; process until smooth. Pour into 10 glasses; sprinkle with ground nutmeg.

Makes 10 (½-cup) servings

Clown Cupcakes

Makes 12 clown cupcakes

- **1 package DUNCAN HINES® Moist Deluxe Yellow Cake Mix**
- **12 scoops vanilla ice cream**
- **12 sugar ice cream cones**
- **1 container (7 ounces) refrigerated aerosol whipped cream**
- **Assorted colored decors**
- **Assorted candies for eyes, nose and mouth**

1. Preheat oven to 350°F. Place 2½-inch paper liners in 24 muffin cups.

2. Prepare, bake and cool cupcakes following package directions.

3. Remove paper from cupcakes. Place top-side down on serving plates. Top with scoops of ice cream. Place cones on ice cream for hats. Spray whipped cream around bottom of cupcakes for collar. Spray three small dots up front on cones. Decorate faces with assorted colored decors.

Note: Freeze remaining cupcakes for later use.

Purple Cow Jumped Over the Moon

Mini Pizza Cookies

Makes 8 cookies

- **1 20-ounce tube prepared sugar cookie dough**
- **2 cups (16 ounces) prepared pink frosting**
- **"M&M's"® Chocolate Mini Baking Bits**
- **"Pizza" toppings**

Preheat oven to 350°F. Lightly grease cookie sheets; set aside. Divide dough into 8 equal portions. On lightly floured surface, roll each portion of dough into ¼-inch-thick circle; place about 2 inches apart onto prepared cookie sheets. Bake 10 to 13 minutes or until golden brown on edges. Cool completely on wire racks. Spread top of each pizza with frosting; sprinkle with "M&M's"® Chocolate Mini Baking Bits and 2 or 3 "pizza" toppings.

Rainbows

Makes about 5 dozen cookies

- **2¼ cups all-purpose flour**
- **¼ teaspoon salt**
- **1 cup sugar**
- **¾ cup butter, softened**
- **1 egg**
- **1 teaspoon vanilla**
- **1 teaspoon almond extract**
- **Red, green, yellow and blue paste food colors**
- **White frosting and yellow sugar sprinkles**

Combine flour and salt. Beat sugar and butter in large bowl until fluffy. Beat in egg, vanilla and extract. Add flour mixture. Beat until well blended. Divide dough into 10 equal sections.

Blend 4 sections dough and red food color, 3 sections dough and green food color, 2 sections dough and yellow food color, and remaining dough and blue food color. Refrigerate 30 minutes.

Shape blue dough into 8-inch log. Shape yellow dough into 8×3-inch rectangle; place on waxed paper. Place blue log in center of yellow rectangle. Fold yellow edges up and around blue log, pinching to seal. Roll to form smooth log.

Roll green dough into 8×5-inch rectangle on waxed paper. Place yellow log in center of green rectangle. Fold green edges up and around yellow log. Pinch to seal. Roll gently to form smooth log. Roll red dough into 8×7-inch rectangle. Place green log in center of red rectangle. Fold red edges up and around green log. Pinch to seal. Roll gently to form smooth log. Wrap in plastic wrap. Refrigerate 1 hour.

Preheat oven to 350°F. Grease cookie sheets. Cut log in half lengthwise. Cut each half into ¼-inch-thick slices. Place slices 1 inch apart on prepared cookie sheets. Bake 8 to 12 minutes. *(Do not brown.)* Cool on cookie sheets 1 minute. Remove to wire racks; cool completely. Pipe small amount of frosting on each cookie; sprinkle with sugar.

Mini Pizza Cookies

It's Snack Time

One Potato, Two Potato

Having a tough time getting your child to eat enough potatoes? After sampling these crispy low-fat potato wedges, the kids will be begging for more!

Makes 4 servings

Nonstick cooking spray
2 medium baking potatoes, cut lengthwise into 4 wedges
Salt
½ cup unseasoned dry bread crumbs
2 tablespoons grated Parmesan cheese (optional)
1½ teaspoons dried oregano leaves, dill weed, Italian herbs or paprika
Spicy brown or honey mustard, ketchup or reduced-fat sour cream

1. Preheat oven to 425°F. Spray baking sheet with nonstick cooking spray; set aside.

2. Spray cut sides of potatoes generously with cooking spray; sprinkle lightly with salt.

3. Combine bread crumbs, Parmesan cheese and desired herb in shallow dish. Add potatoes; toss lightly until potatoes are generously coated with crumb mixture. Place on prepared baking sheet.

4. Bake potatoes until browned and tender, about 20 minutes. Serve warm as dippers with mustard.

Potato Sweets: Omit Parmesan cheese, herbs and mustard. Substitute sweet potatoes for baking potatoes. Cut and spray potatoes as directed; coat generously with desired amount of cinnamon-sugar. Bake as directed. Serve warm as dippers with peach or pineapple preserves or honey mustard.

One Potato, Two Potato

Tex-Mex Chicken Fingers

Makes 12 appetizers

½ cup dried bread crumbs or cracker crumbs
2 tablespoons all-purpose flour
1 teaspoon chili powder
½ teaspoon salt
¼ teaspoon ground cumin
1 pound (about 12) boneless chicken tenderloins
2 eggs, lightly beaten
3 to 4 tablespoons vegetable oil
ORTEGA® Green Chile Picante Sauce, mild

COMBINE crumbs, flour, chili powder, salt and cumin in small shallow bowl.

DIP chicken in eggs; coat with crumb mixture.

HEAT oil in large skillet over medium-high heat. Add chicken; cook for 5 to 6 minutes or until golden brown on outside and no longer pink in center. Serve with picante sauce for dipping.

Bite-Size Tacos

Makes 8 appetizer servings

1 pound ground beef
1 package (1.25 ounces) taco seasoning mix
¾ cup water
1⅓ cups (2.8-ounce can) FRENCH'S® French Fried Onions, divided
¼ cup chopped fresh cilantro
32 bite-size round tortilla chips
¾ cup low-fat sour cream
⅓ cup shredded Cheddar cheese

Preheat oven to 350°F. Prepare taco mixture according to package directions using ground beef, seasoning mix and water. Stir in *⅔ cup* French Fried Onions and cilantro.

Arrange tortilla chips on foil-lined baking sheet. Spread each chip with 1 tablespoon beef mixture and 1 teaspoon sour cream. Sprinkle evenly with cheese and remaining *⅔ cup* onions.

Bake 5 minutes or until cheese melts and onions are golden.

Prep Time: 20 minutes
Cook Time: 15 minutes

Tex-Mex Chicken Fingers

Nachos à la Ortega®

Makes 4 to 6 servings

1¾ cups (1-pound can) ORTEGA® Refried Beans, heated
4 cups (4 ounces) tortilla chips
1½ cups (6 ounces) shredded Cheddar or Monterey Jack cheese
¼ cup ORTEGA® Sliced Jalapeños
ORTEGA® Thick & Chunky Salsa, hot, medium or mild
Sour cream
Additional topping suggestions: guacamole, sliced ripe olives, chopped green onions, chopped fresh cilantro

SPREAD beans onto bottom of large ovenproof platter or jelly-roll pan. Arrange chips over beans. Top with cheese and jalapeños.

PLACE under preheated broiler, 4 inches from heat source, for 1 to 1½ minutes or until cheese is melted. Top with salsa, sour cream and additional toppings, if desired.

Baked Mozzarella Sticks

Makes 12 cheese sticks

Butter-flavored nonstick cooking spray
12 ounces (2 blocks) ALPINE LACE® Fat Free Pasteurized Process Skim Milk Cheese Product—For Mozzarella Lovers
½ cup egg substitute or 2 large eggs
1 cup Italian seasoned dry bread crumbs
¼ cup minced fresh parsley

1. Preheat the oven to 400°F. Spray 2 large baking sheets with the cooking spray.

2. Cut each block of cheese in half crosswise, then each half lengthwise into 3 equal sticks (about 3×¾ inches), making a total of 12 sticks.

3. In a medium-size bowl, whisk the egg substitute (or the whole eggs) until frothy. On a plate, toss the bread crumbs with the parsley.

4. Dip each cheese stick first into the egg substitute, then roll in the bread crumbs, pressing them slightly as you go. Arrange the cheese in a single layer on the baking sheets.

5. Spray the sticks lightly with the cooking spray. Bake for 10 minutes or until golden brown and crispy.

Nachos à la Ortega®

Soft Pretzels

Makes 8 servings

1 package (16 ounces) hot roll mix plus ingredients to prepare mix
1 egg white
2 teaspoons water
2 tablespoons *each* assorted coatings: grated Parmesan cheese, sesame seeds, poppy seeds, dried oregano leaves

1. Prepare hot roll mix according to package directions.

2. Preheat oven to 375°F. Spray baking sheets with nonstick cooking spray; set aside.

3. Divide dough equally into 16 pieces; roll each piece with hands to form a rope, 7 to 10 inches long. Place on prepared cookie sheets; form into desired shape (hearts, wreaths, pretzels, snails, loops, etc.).

4. Beat together egg white and water in small bowl until foamy. Brush onto dough shapes; sprinkle each shape with 1½ teaspoons of one of the coatings.

5. Bake until golden brown, about 15 minutes. Serve warm or at room temperature.

Fruit Twists: Omit coatings. Prepare dough and roll into ropes as directed. Place ropes on lightly floured surface. Roll out, or pat, each rope into rectangle, ¼ inch thick; brush each rectangle with about 1 teaspoon spreadable fruit or preserves. Fold each rectangle lengthwise in half; twist into desired shape. Bake as directed.

Cheese Twists: Omit coatings. Prepare dough and roll into rectangles as directed in Fruit Twists. Sprinkle each rectangle with about 1 tablespoon shredded Cheddar or other flavor cheese. Fold dough rectangles, shape and bake as directed for Fruit Twists.

Take-Along Snack Mix

Makes about 3½ cups

1 tablespoon butter or margarine
2 tablespoons honey
1 cup toasted oat cereal, any flavor
½ cup coarsely broken pecans
½ cup thin pretzel sticks, broken in half
½ cup raisins
1 cup "M&M's"® Chocolate Mini Baking Bits

In large heavy skillet over low heat, melt butter; add honey and stir until blended. Add cereal, nuts, pretzels and raisins, stirring until all pieces are evenly coated. Continue cooking over low heat about 10 minutes, stirring frequently. Remove from heat; immediately spread on waxed paper until cool. Add "M&M's"® Chocolate Mini Baking Bits. Store in tightly covered container.

Soft Pretzels

Picnic Pizza Biscuits

Makes 10 servings

- **1 can (10 ounces) refrigerated buttermilk biscuits**
- **1 pound hot Italian sausage, casings removed**
- **½ cup chopped onion**
- **½ cup sliced mushrooms**
- **½ cup chopped green bell pepper**
- **½ cup (2 ounces) shredded mozzarella cheese**
- **¼ cup marinara or pizza sauce**
- **2 tablespoons FRENCH'S® Dijon Mustard**

1. Preheat oven to 375°F. Separate biscuits; pat or roll into 10 (4-inch) circles on floured surface. Press circles into 12-cup muffin pan.

2. Cook sausage in large nonstick skillet over high heat 5 minutes or until browned, stirring to separate meat; drain fat. Add onion, mushrooms and bell pepper; cook and stir 3 minutes or until vegetables are tender. Stir in cheese, sauce and mustard; mix well.

3. Mound filling evenly in biscuits. Bake 20 minutes or until biscuits are browned. Serve warm or at room temperature.

Prep Time: 30 minutes
Cook Time: 25 minutes

Buffalo Bar-B-Q Nuggets

Makes 6 to 8 servings

- **½ cup *Frank's® RedHot®* Sauce**
- **⅓ cup butter, melted**
- **1½ pounds boneless skinless chicken thighs or breasts**
- **Lettuce leaves**
- **Blue cheese salad dressing (optional)**

1. Combine ***RedHot*** Sauce and butter in small bowl; mix well. Reserve ⅓ cup sauce mixture. Pour remaining sauce over chicken. Cover; refrigerate 20 minutes. Prepare grill.

2. Remove chicken; discard remaining marinade. Place chicken on oiled grid. Grill, over medium coals, about 10 minutes or until no longer pink in center. Heat reserved sauce. Cut chicken into bite-size pieces; toss chicken pieces in warmed sauce.

3. Arrange chicken on lettuce-lined serving platter. Serve with blue cheese dressing, if desired.

Prep Time: 10 minutes
Marinate Time: 20 minutes
Cook Time: 10 minutes

Picnic Pizza Biscuits

Pizza Bread Sticks

Makes 14 servings

1 package (¼ ounce) active dry yeast
¾ cup warm water (105°F to 115°F)
2½ cups all-purpose flour
½ cup (2 ounces) shredded part-skim mozzarella cheese
¼ cup (1 ounce) shredded Parmesan cheese
¼ cup chopped red bell pepper
1 green onion with top, sliced
1 medium clove garlic, minced
½ teaspoon dried basil leaves, crushed
½ teaspoon dried oregano leaves, crushed
¼ teaspoon crushed hot red pepper (optional)
¼ teaspoon salt
1 tablespoon olive oil

1. Preheat oven to 400°F. Spray 2 large nonstick baking sheets with nonstick cooking spray; set aside.

2. Sprinkle yeast over warm water in 1-cup measuring cup or small bowl; stir until yeast dissolves. Let stand 5 minutes or until bubbly.

3. Meanwhile, place all remaining ingredients except oil in food processor; process a few seconds to combine. With food processor running, gradually add yeast mixture and oil. Process just until mixture forms a ball. (Add an additional 2 tablespoons flour if dough is too sticky.)

4. Transfer dough to lightly floured surface; knead 1 minute. Let dough rest 5 minutes. Roll out dough with lightly floured rolling pin to form 14×8-inch rectangle; cut dough crosswise into ½-inch-wide strips. Twist dough strips; place on prepared baking sheets.

5. Bake 14 to 16 minutes or until lightly browned.

Cookie Dough Fun

Cookie Dough Fun

COOKIE DOUGH FUN

Simple Pleasures

"Everything but the Kitchen Sink" Bar Cookies

What you need:

1 package (18 ounces) refrigerated chocolate chip cookie dough
1 jar (7 ounces) marshmallow creme
½ cup creamy peanut butter
1½ cups toasted corn cereal
½ cup miniature candy-coated chocolate pieces

1 Preheat oven to 350°F. Grease 13×9-inch baking pan. Remove dough from wrapper according to package directions.

2 Press dough into prepared baking pan. Bake 13 minutes.

3 Remove baking pan from oven. Drop teaspoonfuls of marshmallow creme and peanut butter over hot cookie base.

4 Bake 1 minute. Carefully spread marshmallow creme and peanut butter over cookie base.

5 Sprinkle cereal and chocolate pieces over melted marshmallow and peanut butter mixture.

6 Bake 7 minutes. Cool completely on wire rack. Cut into 2-inch bars.

Makes 3 dozen bar cookies

"Everything but the Kitchen Sink" Bar Cookies

Sandwich Cookies

What you need:

1 package (20 ounces) refrigerated cookie dough, any flavor
All-purpose flour (optional)

FILLINGS
Any combination of colored frostings, peanut butter or assorted ice creams

DECORATIONS
Colored sprinkles, chocolate-covered raisins, miniature candy-coated chocolate pieces and other assorted small candies

1 Preheat oven to 350°F. Grease cookie sheets.

2 Remove dough from wrapper according to package directions.

3 Cut dough into 4 equal sections. Reserve 1 section; refrigerate remaining 3 sections.

4 Roll reserved dough to ¼-inch thickness. Sprinkle with flour to minimize sticking, if necessary.

5 Cut out cookies using 1 (¾-inch) round cookie cutter. Transfer cookies to prepared cookie sheets, placing about 2 inches apart. Repeat steps with remaining dough.

6 Bake 8 to 11 minutes or until edges are lightly browned. Remove to wire racks; cool completely.

7 To make sandwich, spread about 1 tablespoon desired filling to within ¼ inch of the underside of 1 cookie. Top with second cookie, pressing gently.

8 Roll side of sandwich in desired decorations. Repeat with remaining cookies.

Makes about 20 to 24 sandwich cookies

Tip

Be creative—make sandwich cookies using 2 or more flavors of refrigerated cookie dough. Mix and match to see how many flavor combinations you can come up with.

Chocolate Malted Cookies

What you need:

½ cup butter, softened
½ cup shortening
1¾ cups powdered sugar, divided
1 teaspoon vanilla
2 cups all-purpose flour
1 cup malted milk powder, divided
¼ cup unsweetened cocoa powder

1 Beat butter, shortening, ¾ cup powdered sugar and vanilla in large bowl at high speed of electric mixer.

2 Add flour, ½ cup malted milk powder and cocoa; beat at low speed until well blended. Refrigerate several hours or overnight.

3 Preheat oven to 350°F. Shape slightly mounded teaspoonfuls of dough into balls.

4 Place dough balls about 2 inches apart on ungreased cookie sheets.

5 Bake 14 to 16 minutes or until lightly browned.

6 Meanwhile, combine remaining 1 cup powdered sugar and ½ cup malted milk powder in medium bowl.

7 Remove cookies to wire racks; cool 5 minutes. Roll cookies in powdered sugar mixture.

Makes about 4 dozen cookies

Tip

Substitute 6 ounces melted semisweet chocolate for the 1 cup powdered sugar and ½ cup malted milk powder used to roll the cookies. Instead, dip cookies in melted chocolate and let dry on wire racks until coating is set.

Peanuts

What you need:

½ cup butter, softened
¼ cup shortening
¼ cup creamy peanut butter
1 cup powdered sugar, sifted
1 egg yolk
1 teaspoon vanilla
1¾ cups all-purpose flour
1 cup finely ground honey-roasted peanuts, divided
Peanut Buttery Frosting (recipe follows)

1 Grease cookie sheets.

2 Beat butter, shortening and peanut butter in large bowl at medium speed of electric mixer. Gradually add powdered sugar, beating until smooth. Add egg yolk and vanilla; beat well. Add flour; mix well. Stir in ⅓ cup ground peanuts. Cover dough; refrigerate 1 hour.

3 Prepare Peanut Buttery Frosting. Preheat oven to 350°F. Shape dough into 1-inch balls. Place 2 balls, side by side and slightly touching, on prepared cookie sheet. Gently flatten balls with fingertips and form into "peanut" shape. Repeat steps with remaining dough.

4 Bake 16 to 18 minutes or until edges are lightly browned. Cool on cookie sheets 5 minutes. Remove cookies to wire racks; cool completely.

5 Place remaining ⅔ cup ground peanuts in shallow dish. Spread about 2 teaspoons Peanut Buttery Frosting evenly over top of each cookie. Coat with ground peanuts.

Makes about 2 dozen cookies

Peanut Buttery Frosting

½ cup butter or margarine, softened
½ cup creamy peanut butter
2 cups powdered sugar, sifted
½ teaspoon vanilla
3 to 6 tablespoons milk

1 Beat butter and peanut butter in medium bowl at medium speed of electric mixer until smooth. Gradually add powdered sugar and vanilla until blended but crumbly.

2 Add milk, 1 tablespoon at a time, until smooth. Refrigerate until ready to use.

Makes 1⅓ cups frosting

Butter Pretzel Cookies

What you need:

1 recipe Butter Cookie Dough (page 158)

TOPPINGS

White, rainbow or colored rock or coarse sugar

1 Prepare Butter Cookie Dough. Cover; refrigerate about 4 hours or until firm.

2 Preheat oven to 350°F. Grease cookie sheets.

3 Divide dough into 4 equal sections. Reserve 1 section; refrigerate remaining 3 sections. Divide reserved dough into 4 equal pieces. Roll each dough piece on lightly floured surface to 12-inch rope; sprinkle with rock or coarse sugar.

4 Transfer 1 rope at a time to prepared cookie sheets. Form each rope into pretzel shape. Repeat steps with remaining dough pieces.

5 Bake 14 to 18 minutes or until edges begin to brown. Cool cookies on cookie sheets 1 minute. Remove to wire racks; cool completely.

Makes 16 cookies

Chocolate Pretzel Cookies

What you need:

1 recipe Chocolate Cookie Dough (page 158)

TOPPINGS

White and colored rock or coarse sugar

1 Prepare Chocolate Cookie Dough. Cover; refrigerate about 2 hours or until firm.

2 Preheat oven to 325°F. Grease cookie sheets.

3 Divide dough into 4 equal sections. Reserve 1 section; refrigerate remaining 3 sections. Divide reserved dough into 5 equal pieces. Roll each dough piece on lightly floured surface to 12-inch rope; sprinkle with rock or coarse sugar.

4 Transfer 1 rope at a time to prepared cookie sheets. Form each rope into pretzel shape. Repeat steps with remaining dough pieces.

5 Bake 12 to 14 minutes or until edges begin to brown. Cool cookies on cookie sheets 1 minute. Remove to wire racks; cool completely.

Makes 20 cookies

Butter Pretzel Cookies, Chocolate Pretzel Cookies

Surprise Cookies

What you need:

1 package (20 ounces) refrigerated sugar cookie dough
All-purpose flour (optional)

FILLINGS

Any combination of walnut halves, whole almonds, chocolate-covered raisins or caramel candy squares

1 Grease cookie sheets. Remove dough from wrapper according to package directions.

2 Cut dough into 4 equal sections. Reserve 1 section; refrigerate remaining 3 sections.

3 Roll reserved dough to ¼-inch thickness. Sprinkle with flour to minimize sticking, if necessary.

4 Cut out 3-inch square cookie with sharp knife. Transfer cookie to prepared cookie sheet.

5 Place desired "surprise" filling in center of cookie. (If using caramel candy square, place so that caramel forms diamond shape within square.)

6 Bring up 4 corners of dough towards center; pinch gently to seal. Repeat steps with remaining dough and fillings, placing cookies about 2 inches apart.

7 Freeze cookies 20 minutes. Preheat oven to 350°F.

8 Bake 9 to 11 minutes or until edges are lightly browned. Remove to wire racks; cool completely.

Makes about 14 cookies

Tip

Make extra batches of these simple cookies and store in freezer in heavy-duty freezer bags. Take out a few at a time for kids' after-school treats.

Fruity Cookie Rings and Twists

What you need:

1 package (20 ounces) refrigerated sugar cookie dough
3 cups fruit-flavored cereal, crushed, divided

1 Remove dough from wrapper according to package directions.

2 Combine dough and ½ cup cereal in large bowl. Divide dough into 32 balls. Refrigerate 1 hour.

3 Preheat oven to 375°F. Roll dough balls into 6- to 8-inch-long ropes. Roll ropes in remaining cereal to coat; shape into rings or fold in half and twist.

4 Place cookies 2 inches apart on ungreased cookie sheets.

5 Bake 10 to 11 minutes or until lightly browned. Remove to wire racks; cool completely.

Makes 32 cookies

Tip

These cookie rings can be transformed into Christmas tree ornaments by poking a hole in the unbaked ring using a drinking straw. Bake cookies and decorate with colored gels and small candies to resemble wreaths. Loop thin ribbon through holes and tie together.

Pecan Toffee Filled Ravioli Cookies

What you need:

1 cup packed brown sugar
¼ cup butter, melted
½ cup chopped pecans
2 tablespoons all-purpose flour
2 recipes Butter Cookie Dough (page 158)

1 Stir brown sugar into melted butter in large bowl until well blended. Add pecans and flour; mix well.

2 Transfer filling to waxed paper; shape into 7-inch square.

3 Cut into 36 (1¼-inch) pieces. Refrigerate 1 hour or overnight.

4 Prepare Butter Cookie Dough. Cover; refrigerate about 4 hours or until firm. Roll half of dough on well-floured sheet of waxed paper to 12-inch square.

5 Repeat with second half of dough. If dough becomes soft, refrigerate 1 hour.

6 Preheat oven to 350°F. Lightly score 1 layer of dough at 2-inch intervals to form 36 squares.

7 Place 1 square of brown sugar filling in center of each square.

8 Carefully place second layer of dough over brown sugar mixture. Press gently between rows. Cut with knife, ravioli wheel or pastry cutter.

9 Transfer filled ravioli to ungreased cookie sheets.

10 Bake 14 to 16 minutes or until lightly browned. Cool on cookie sheets 5 minutes. Remove to wire racks; cool completely.

Makes 3 dozen cookies

Tip

For a fun flavor adventure, fill ravioli cookies with 1-inch squares of semisweet or milk chocolate instead of brown sugar-pecan mixture. Omit steps 1 through 3.

Peanut Butter and Chocolate Spirals

What you need:

1 package (20 ounces) refrigerated sugar cookie dough
1 package (20 ounces) refrigerated peanut butter cookie dough
¼ cup unsweetened cocoa powder
⅓ cup peanut butter-flavored chips, chopped
¼ cup all-purpose flour
⅓ cup miniature chocolate chips

1 Remove each dough from wrapper according to package directions.

2 Place sugar cookie dough and cocoa in large bowl; mix with fork to blend. Stir in peanut butter chips.

3 Place peanut butter cookie dough and flour in another large bowl; mix with fork to blend. Stir in chocolate chips. Divide each dough in half; refrigerate 1 hour.

4 Roll each dough on floured surface to 6×12-inch rectangle. Layer each half of peanut butter dough onto each half of chocolate dough. Roll up dough, starting at long end to form 2 (12-inch) rolls. Refrigerate 1 hour.

5 Preheat oven to 375°F. Cut dough into ½-inch-thick slices. Place cookies 2 inches apart on ungreased cookie sheets.

6 Bake 10 to 12 minutes or until lightly browned. Remove to wire racks; cool completely.

Makes 4 dozen cookies

Apple Pie Wedges

What you need:

1 cup butter, softened
⅔ cup sugar
1 egg yolk
⅓ cup apple butter
2⅓ cups all-purpose flour
1 teaspoon ground cinnamon
½ teaspoon apple pie spice
½ teaspoon vanilla

1 Beat butter and sugar in medium bowl at medium speed of electric mixer until fluffy.

2 Add egg yolk and apple butter; mix well. Add flour, cinnamon, apple pie spice and vanilla; beat at low speed until well blended.

3 Divide dough in half. Shape each half into a 6-inch disc on waxed paper. Refrigerate 30 minutes.

4 Preheat oven to 325°F. Invert 1 disc of dough into ungreased 9-inch round pie plate.

5 Press dough into plate with lightly floured hand covering plate completely.

6 Flute edges using handle of wooden spoon. Deeply score into 8 wedges.

7 Prick surface using tines of fork. Repeat steps with remaining disc of dough and another pie plate.

8 Bake 35 minutes or until golden brown. Remove to wire rack; cool completely. Cut into wedges.

Makes 16 wedges

Tip

Serve these tasty cookies warm with a big scoop of vanilla or cinnamon-flavored ice cream.

Kids in the Kitchen

Kids' Cookie Dough

What you need:

1 cup butter, softened
2 teaspoons vanilla
½ cup powdered sugar
2¼ cups all-purpose flour
¼ teaspoon salt

DECORATIONS

Assorted colored glazes, frostings, sugars and small candies

1 Preheat oven to 350°F. Grease cookie sheets.

2 Beat butter and vanilla in large bowl at high speed of electric mixer until fluffy. Add sugar and beat at medium speed until blended.

3 Combine flour and salt in small bowl. Gradually add to butter mixture.

4 Divide dough into 10 equal sections. Form shapes directly on prepared cookie sheets according to photo, or as desired, for each section.

5 Bake 15 to 18 minutes or until edges are lightly browned. Cool completely on cookie sheets.

6 Decorate with glazes, frostings, sugars and small candies as desired.

Makes 10 (4-inch) cookies

Kids' Cookie Dough

Diamond Backs

What you need:

1 recipe Gingerbread Cookie Dough (page 157)

DECORATIONS

2 egg yolks
½ teaspoon water
Assorted paste food colors

SUPPLIES

Small craft paint brushes

1 Prepare Gingerbread Cookie Dough. Cover; refrigerate about 8 hours or until firm.

2 Combine egg yolks and water in small bowl. Divide egg mixture evenly among small custard cups. Add different food colors to each cup; blend well. Set aside.

3 Preheat oven to 350°F. Grease cookie sheets.

4 Divide dough in half. Reserve 1 half; refrigerate remaining dough. Roll reserved dough into rectangle on floured surface to ¼-inch thickness.

5 Cut dough into squiggly 8×1-inch strips for bodies, leaving one end pointed. Carefully transfer to prepared cookie sheets.

6 Reroll scraps to ¼-inch thickness; cut into 1½-inch teardrop shapes for heads.

7 Paint bodies of diamond backs as desired using small craft paint brushes and egg yolk paint.

8 Place teardrop heads on bodies; press gently. Decorate according to photo or as desired. Repeat with remaining dough.

9 Bake 12 to 13 minutes or until set. Cool on cookie sheets 5 minutes. Remove to wire racks; cool completely.

Makes about 14 cookies

Tip

Using paste food color for diamond backs is not absolutely necessary, but it can give better results by producing bright vibrant hues. Also, it will not thin the egg yolk mixture like liquid food color.

Cookie Canvases

What you need:

1 package (20 ounces) refrigerated cookie dough, any flavor
All-purpose flour (optional)
1 recipe Cookie Glaze (page 160)

SUPPLIES

1 (3½-inch) square cardboard template
1 (2½×4½-inch) rectangular cardboard template
Assorted liquid food colors
Small craft paint brushes

1 Preheat oven to 350°F. Grease cookie sheets.

2 Remove dough from wrapper according to package directions. Cut dough in half. Wrap half of dough in plastic wrap and refrigerate.

3 Roll remaining dough on floured surface to ¼-inch thickness. Sprinkle with flour to minimize sticking, if necessary. Cut out cookie shapes using cardboard templates as guides. Place cookies 2 inches apart on prepared cookie sheets. Repeat steps with remaining dough.

4 Bake 8 to 10 minutes or until edges are lightly browned. Remove from oven and straighten cookie edges with spatula. Cool cookies completely on cookie sheets. Prepare Cookie Glaze.

5 Place cookies on wire racks set over waxed paper. Drizzle Cookie Glaze over cookies. Let stand at room temperature 40 minutes or until glaze is set. Place food colors in small bowls. Using small craft paint brushes, decorate cookies with food colors by "painting" designs such as rainbows, flowers and animals.

Makes 8 to 10 cookie canvases

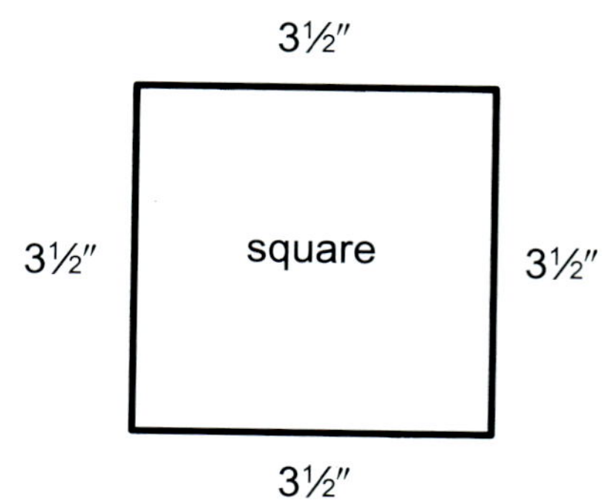

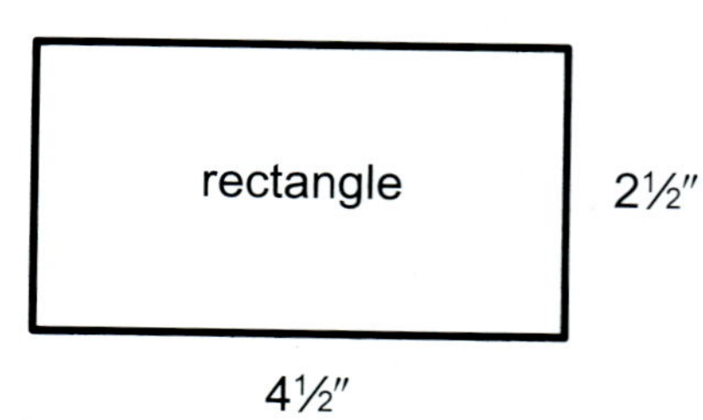

1 TABLESPOON

Cookie Clocks

What you need:

1 package (20 ounces) refrigerated cookie dough, any flavor
All-purpose flour (optional)

DECORATIONS

Colored and white frostings and assorted candies

1 Preheat oven to 350°F. Grease cookie sheets.

2 Remove dough from wrapper according to package directions. Cut dough into 4 equal sections. Reserve 1 section; refrigerate remaining 3 sections. Sprinkle reserved dough with flour to minimize sticking, if necessary. Roll dough to ¼-inch thickness.

3 Cut out various shapes of clocks and watches using diagrams as guides. Carefully place cookies 2 inches apart on prepared cookie sheets. Repeat steps with remaining dough.

4 Bake 8 to 10 minutes or until edges are lightly browned. Cool cookies on cookie sheets 5 minutes. Remove to wire racks; cool completely. Decorate as desired.

Makes about 8 to 10 cookies

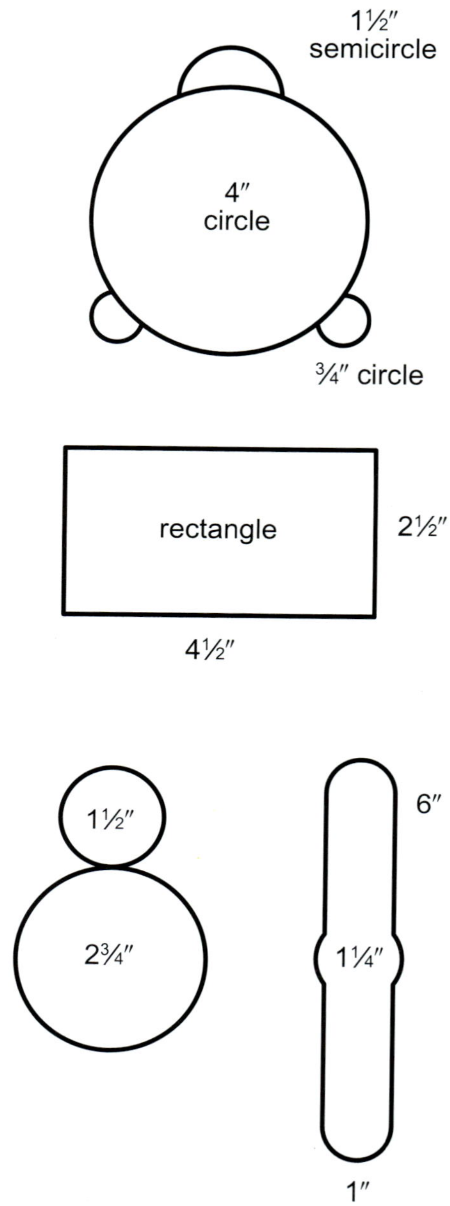

11:35

Handprints

What you need:

1 package (20 ounces) refrigerated cookie dough, any flavor
All-purpose flour (optional)

DECORATIONS
Cookie glazes, frostings, nondairy whipped topping, peanut butter and assorted candies

1. Grease cookie sheets.

2. Remove dough from wrapper according to package directions.

3. Cut dough into 4 equal sections. Reserve 1 section; refrigerate remaining 3 sections. Sprinkle reserved dough with flour to minimize sticking, if necessary.

4. Roll dough on prepared cookie sheet to 5×7-inch rectangle.

5. Place hand, palm-side down, on dough. Carefully, cut around outline of hand with knife. Remove scraps. Separate fingers as much as possible using small spatula. Pat fingers outward to lengthen slightly. Repeat steps with remaining dough.

6. Freeze dough 15 minutes. Preheat oven to 350°F.

7. Bake 7 to 13 minutes or until cookies are set and edges are golden brown. Cool completely on cookie sheets.

8. Decorate as desired.

Makes 5 adult handprint cookies

Tip

To get the kids involved, let them use their hands to make the handprints. Be sure that an adult is available to cut around the outline with a knife. The kids will enjoy seeing how their handprints bake into big cookies.

Chocolate Teddy Bears

What you need:

1 recipe Chocolate Cookie Dough (page 158)

DECORATIONS

White and colored frostings, decorator gels, coarse sugars and assorted small candies

1 Prepare Chocolate Cookie Dough. Cover; refrigerate about 2 hours or until firm.

2 Preheat oven to 325°F. Grease cookie sheets.

3 Divide dough in half. Reserve 1 half; refrigerate remaining dough.

4 Divide reserved dough into 8 equal balls. Cut 1 ball in half; roll 1 half into ball for body.

5 Cut other half into 2 equal pieces; roll 1 piece into 4 small balls for paws.

6 Divide second piece into thirds. Roll two-thirds of dough into ball for head.

7 Divide remaining one-third of dough in half; roll into 2 small balls for ears.

8 Place balls together directly on prepared cookie sheet to form bear according to diagram. Repeat steps with remaining dough.

9 Bake 13 to 15 minutes or until set. Cool completely on cookie sheets. Decorate with frostings, gels, sugars and assorted candies as desired.

Makes 16 (4-inch) teddy bears

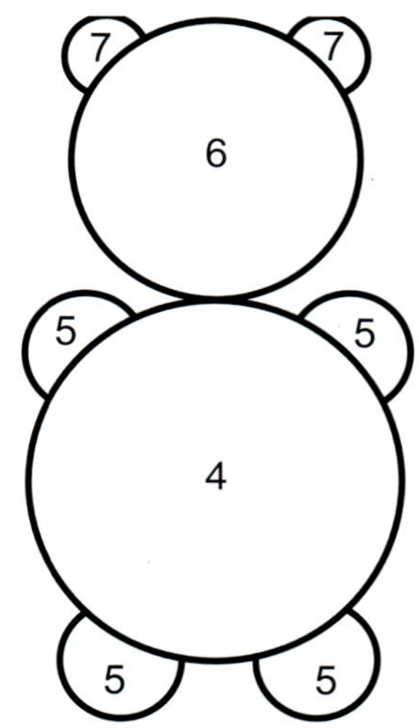

Numbers in diagram refer to steps in recipe.

Puzzle Cookie

What you need:

- ¾ cup shortening
- ½ cup packed light brown sugar
- 6 tablespoons dark molasses
- 2 egg whites
- ¾ teaspoon vanilla
- 2¼ cups all-purpose flour
- ¾ teaspoon baking soda
- ¼ teaspoon plus ⅛ teaspoon baking powder
- ¾ teaspoon salt
- 2 teaspoons ground cinnamon
- ¾ teaspoon ground ginger

DECORATIONS

- Assorted colored frostings, colored sugars, colored decorator gels and assorted small candies

1 Beat shortening, brown sugar, molasses, egg whites and vanilla in large bowl at high speed of electric mixer until smooth.

2 Combine flour, baking soda, baking powder, salt, cinnamon and ginger in medium bowl. Add to shortening mixture; mix well. Shape dough into flat rectangle. Wrap in plastic wrap and refrigerate about 8 hours or until firm.

3 Preheat oven to 350°F. Grease jelly-roll pan.

4 Sprinkle dough with additional flour. Place dough in center of prepared pan and roll evenly to within ½ inch of edge of pan. Cut shapes into dough according to photo, using cookie cutters or free-hand, allowing at least 1 inch between each shape. Cut through dough using sharp knife, but do not remove cookie shapes.

5 Bake 12 minutes or until edges begin to brown lightly. Remove from oven and retrace shapes with knife. Return to oven 5 to 6 minutes. Cool in pan 5 minutes. Carefully remove shapes to wire racks; cool completely.

6 Decorate shapes with frostings, sugars, decorator gels and small candies as shown in photo. Leave puzzle frame in pan. Decorate with frostings, colored sugars and gels to represent sky, clouds, grass and water, if desired. Return shapes to their respective openings to complete puzzle.

Makes 1 (15×10-inch) puzzle cookie

Novel Ideas

Critters-in-Holes

What you need:

48 chewy caramel candies coated in milk chocolate
48 pieces candy corn
Miniature candy-coated chocolate pieces
1 container frosting, any flavor
1 package (20 ounces) refrigerated peanut butter cookie dough

1 Cut slit into side of 1 caramel candy using sharp knife.

2 Carefully insert 1 piece candy corn into slit. Repeat with remaining caramel candies and candy corn.

3 Attach miniature chocolate pieces to caramel candies to resemble "eyes" using frosting as glue. Decorate as desired.

4 Preheat oven to 350°F. Grease 12 (1¾-inch) muffin cups.

5 Remove dough from wrapper according to package directions. Cut dough into 12 (1-inch) slices. Cut each slice into 4 equal sections. Place 1 section of dough into each muffin cup.

6 Bake 9 minutes. Remove from oven and immediately press 1 decorated caramel candy into center of each cookie. Repeat with remaining ingredients.

7 Remove to wire racks; cool completely.

Makes 4 dozen cookies

Critters-in-Holes

Domino Cookies

What you need:

1 package (20 ounces) refrigerated sugar cookie dough
All-purpose flour (optional)
½ cup semisweet chocolate chips

1 Preheat oven to 350°F. Grease cookie sheets.

2 Remove dough from wrapper according to package directions. Cut dough into 4 equal sections. Reserve 1 section; refrigerate remaining 3 sections.

3 Roll reserved dough to ⅛-inch thickness. Sprinkle with flour to minimize sticking, if necessary.

4 Cut out 9 (1¾×2½-inch) rectangles according to diagram using sharp knife. Place 2 inches apart on prepared cookies sheets.

5 Score each cookie across middle with sharp knife.

6 Gently press chocolate chips, point side down, into dough to resemble various dominos. Repeat with remaining dough and scraps.

7 Bake 8 to 10 minutes or until edges are light golden brown. Remove to wire racks; cool completely.

Makes 36 cookies

Tip

Use these adorable cookies as a learning tool for kids. They can count the number of chocolate chips in each cookie and arrange them in lots of ways: highest to lowest, numerically or even solve simple math problems. As a treat, they can eat the cookies afterwards.

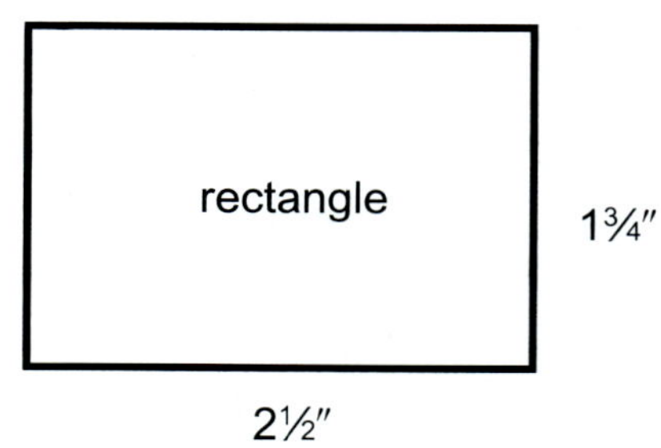

Honey Bees

What you need:

¾ cup shortening
½ cup sugar
¼ cup honey
1 egg
½ teaspoon vanilla
2 cups all-purpose flour
⅓ cup cornmeal
1 teaspoon baking powder
½ teaspoon salt

DECORATIONS

Yellow and black icings or gels and gummy fruit

1 Beat shortening, sugar and honey in large bowl at medium speed of electric mixer until fluffy. Add egg and vanilla; mix until well blended.

2 Combine flour, cornmeal, baking powder and salt in medium bowl. Add to shortening mixture; mix at low speed until well blended.

3 Cover; refrigerate several hours or overnight, if desired.

4 Preheat oven to 375°F. Divide dough into 24 equal sections.

5 Shape each section into oval-shaped ball. Place 2 inches apart on ungreased cookie sheets.

6 Bake 10 to 12 minutes or until lightly browned. Cool 2 minutes on cookie sheets. Remove to wire racks; cool completely.

7 Decorate with icings, gels and gummy fruit to create honey bees.

Makes 2 dozen cookies

Tip

To create a fun summery day, pair these light sweet Honey Bees with a batch of Sunshine Butter Cookies (page 140).

Hot Dog Cookies

What you need:

1 recipe Butter Cookie Dough (page 158)
Liquid food colors
Sesame seeds

TOPPINGS
Shredded coconut, red and green decorator gels, frosting and gummy candies

1 Prepare Butter Cookie Dough. Cover; refrigerate 4 hours or until firm. Grease cookie sheets.

2 Use ⅓ of dough to make "hot dogs." Refrigerate remaining dough. Mix food colors in small bowl to get reddish-brown color following chart on back of food color box. Add reserved ⅓ of dough. Mix color throughout dough using wooden spoon.

3 Divide colored dough into 6 equal sections. Roll each section into thin log shape. Round edges. Set aside.

4 To make "buns," divide remaining dough into 6 equal sections.

5 Roll sections into thick logs. Make very deep indentation the length of log in centers; smooth edges to create buns.

6 Lift buns with small spatula and dip sides in sesame seeds. Place 3 inches apart on prepared cookie sheets.

7 Place hot dogs inside buns.

8 Freeze 20 minutes. Preheat oven to 350°F. Bake 17 to 20 minutes or until bun edges are light golden brown. Cool completely on cookie sheets.

9 Top hot dogs with green-tinted shredded coconut for "relish," white coconut for "onions," red decorator gel for "ketchup" and yellow-tinted frosting or whipped topping for "mustard."

Makes 6 hot dog cookies

Tip

To pipe gels and frosting onto Hot Dog Cookies, you can use a resealable plastic sandwich bag as a substitute for a pastry bag. Fold the top of the bag down to form a cuff and use a spatula to fill bag half full with gel or frosting. Unfold top of bag and a twist down against filling. Snip tiny tip off one corner of bag. Hold top of bag tightly and squeeze filling through opening.

Gingerbread Farm Animals in Corral

What you need:

1 recipe Gingerbread House Dough (page 159)
2 recipes Royal Icing (page 160)

DECORATIONS
Assorted food colors
Shredded coconut
Assorted small hard candies

SUPPLIES
Cardboard
Decorative paper

1 Preheat oven to 375°F. Prepare Gingerbread House Dough. Divide dough into 4 equal sections. To make fence, roll 1 section of dough directly onto large cookie sheet to ¼-inch thickness. Cut into 6 (2¾×6-inch) sections, leaving ½-inch space between sections. Bake 10 to 12 minutes or until edges are browned. Cool completely on wire racks.

2 Roll second section of dough directly onto cookie sheet to ¼-inch thickness. Cut into 4 (2¾×6-inch) sections and 2 (3-inch) sections. Bake 10 to 12 minutes or until edges are browned. Cool completely on wire racks.

3 To make animals, roll remaining 2 sections of dough directly on cookie sheets to ⅛-inch thickness. Cut out animal shapes using animal-shaped cookie cutters. Bake 8 to 12 minutes or until edges are browned. Cool completely on wire racks.

4 Prepare Royal Icing. Tint small amounts of icing with food colors to decorate animals. Place remaining icing in small resealable plastic food storage bag. Cut off small corner of bag for piping.

5 Decorate animals and fence sections with icing and assorted candies according to photo. Cover 20-inch piece of cardboard with decorative paper and plastic wrap. Assemble fence by piping icing on bottom and side edges of fence sections. Use smaller sections to make 2 gates. Pipe icing on feet of animals; arrange so animals can be supported by fence or other animals. Sprinkle green-tinted coconut around feet of animals for grass, if desired.

Makes 1 fence and 2 dozen animals

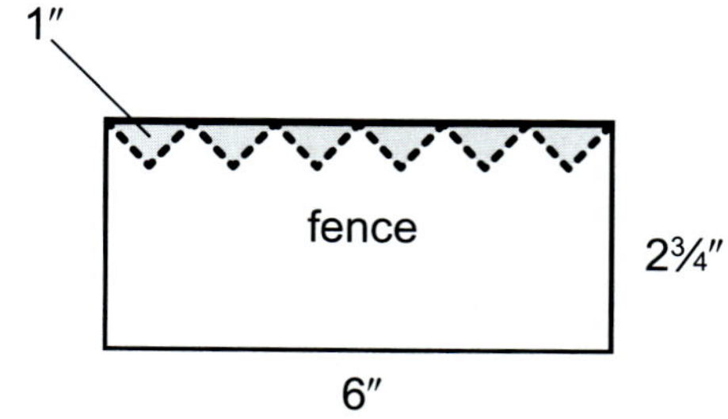

Gingerbread Farm Animals in Corral

Shapers

What you need:

2 packages (20 ounces each) refrigerated sugar cookie dough
Red, yellow, green and blue paste food colors

DECORATIONS

1 container vanilla frosting

1 Remove dough from wrapper according to package directions. Cut each roll of dough in half.

2 Beat ¼ of dough and red food coloring in medium bowl at medium speed of electric mixer until well blended.

3 Roll red dough on sheet of waxed paper to 5-inch log. Set aside.

4 Repeat with remaining dough and food colors. Cover; refrigerate tinted logs 1 hour or until firm.

5 Working with one log at a time, roll on smooth surface to create circular, triangular, square and oval shaped logs. Use ruler to keep triangle and square sides flat.

6 Cover; refrigerate dough 1 hour or until firm.

7 Preheat oven to 350°F. Cut shaped dough into ¼-inch slices. Place 2 inches apart on ungreased baking sheets.

8 Bake 9 to 12 minutes. Remove to wire racks; cool completely.

9 Spoon frosting into resealable plastic food storage bag; seal. Cut tiny tip from corner of bag.

10 Pipe frosting around each cookie to define shape.

Makes about 6½ dozen cookies

Tip

If you have extra liquid food colors at home, tint the vanilla frosting different colors. Frost cookies using contrasting colored frosting, for example green frosting on a red cookie.

VITAMIN D
MILK
HALF PINT (236 ml)

Kaleidoscope Cookies

What you need:

1 package (20 ounces) refrigerated sugar cookie dough
All-purpose flour (optional)
Blue and red liquid food colors
2 tablespoons sprinkles, multi-colored coarse sugar or rock sugar, divided

1 Remove dough from wrapper according to package directions. Cut dough into 5 equal sections. Cover and refrigerate 1 section. Sprinkle remaining 4 sections with flour to minimize sticking, if necessary.

2 Add blue food coloring to 1 section in medium bowl; mix using wooden spoon until well blended. Repeat with another section of dough and red food coloring. Roll each section into 7½-inch log. Cover and refrigerate.

3 Add 1 tablespoon sprinkles to third section in medium bowl; mix using wooden spoon until well blended. Repeat with fourth section of dough and remaining 1 tablespoon sprinkles. Roll each section into 7½-inch log. Cover and refrigerate.

4 Roll reserved section of dough on sheet of waxed paper to 7½×8½-inch rectangle. Place logs of dough in middle of rectangle so that matching colors are diagonal from each other.

5 Bring waxed paper and closest edge of dough up and over top of logs. Press gently. Repeat with opposite side, overlapping dough edges. Press gently. Wrap waxed paper around dough and twist ends to secure.

6 Freeze 20 minutes. Preheat oven to 350°F. Grease cookie sheets.

7 Remove waxed paper. Cut log with sharp knife into ½-inch slices. Place 2 inches apart on prepared cookie sheets.

8 Bake 15 to 17 minutes or until edges are lightly browned. Remove to wire racks; cool completely.

Makes about 15 cookies

Cookie Bowl and Cookie Fruit

What you need:

1 cup butter, softened
1½ cups sugar
2 whole eggs
2 teaspoons grated orange peel
2 teaspoons vanilla
5 cups all-purpose flour
1 teaspoon baking powder
½ teaspoon salt
1 cup sour cream

DECORATIONS

4 egg yolks, divided
4 teaspoons water, divided
Red, yellow, blue and green liquid food colors

SUPPLIES

Small craft paint brushes

1 Beat butter and sugar in large bowl at high speed of electric mixer until light and fluffy. Add whole eggs, orange peel and vanilla; mix until well blended.

2 Combine flour, baking powder and salt in another large bowl. Add half of flour mixture to butter mixture; mix at low speed until well blended. Add sour cream; mix well. Add remaining flour mixture; mix well.

3 Divide dough into 4 equal sections. Cover; refrigerate several hours or overnight.

4 Place 1 egg yolk in each of 4 separate bowls. Add 1 teaspoon water and food color to each; beat lightly. Set aside.

5 Preheat oven to 375°F. Roll 1 section of dough on well-floured surface to 12-inch circle. Carefully transfer to inverted 1½-quart ovenproof bowl. Press overlapping portions of dough together; trim edges. Paint sides of bowl as desired using small craft paint brushes and egg yolk paint.

6 Place bowl on wire rack and then on cookie sheet. Bake 20 to 25 minutes or until lightly browned. Cool completely on bowl.

7 Roll remaining dough on well-floured surface to ⅛-inch thickness. Cut with fruit shaped cookie cutters. Place 2 inches apart on ungreased cookie sheets. Paint as desired with egg yolk paint.

8 Bake 10 to 12 minutes or until edges are lightly browned. Remove to wire racks; cool completely.

Makes 1 bowl and 4 dozen cookies

Baseball Caps

What you need:

1 cup butter, softened
7 ounces almond paste
¾ cup sugar
1 egg
1 teaspoon vanilla
¼ teaspoon salt
3 cups all-purpose flour
Assorted colored icings and colored candies

1 Preheat oven to 350°F. Grease cookie sheets. Beat butter, almond paste, sugar, egg, vanilla and salt in large bowl at high speed of electric mixer until light and fluffy. Add flour all at once; stir just to combine.

2 Roll ¼ of dough on lightly floured surface to ⅛-inch thickness. Cut out 1-inch circles. Place cookies 2 inches apart on prepared cookie sheets.

3 Roll remaining dough into 1-inch balls.* Place one ball on top of half dough circle so about ½ inch of circle sticks out to form bill of baseball cap.

4 Bake 10 to 12 minutes or until lightly browned. If bills brown too quickly, cut small strips of foil and cover with shiny side of foil facing you. Let cool on baking sheet 2 minutes. Remove to wire rack; cool completely. Decorate with icings and candies as shown in photo.

Makes 3 dozen cookies

**Use a 1-tablespoon scoop to keep the baseball caps uniform in size and professional looking.*

Baseball Caps

Twin Oaks

The Thousand Legged Worm

What you need:

1 package (20 ounces) refrigerated sugar cookie dough
2 containers (16 ounces each) chocolate frosting
Black licorice strings, cut into 3-inch pieces
1 marshmallow and coconut-covered chocolate snack cake

DECORATIONS
Miniature round butter cookies and assorted chewy candies

1 Preheat oven to 350°F. Grease cookie sheets.

2 Remove dough from wrapper according to package directions.

3 Cut dough into 30 (½-inch) slices. Place 2 inches apart on prepared cookie sheets.

4 Bake 8 to 10 minutes or until edges are lightly browned. Cool completely on wire racks.

5 Spread underside of 1 cookie with 1 tablespoon frosting. Top with another cookie, pressing gently. Set aside.

6 Spread underside of another cookie with frosting, insert 1 piece of licorice into frosting on each side of cookie and attach to reserved sandwich cookie with frosting.

7 Repeat until 6 cookies are sandwiched together with frosting and licorice.

8 Place cookie stack on its side on serving platter. Repeat with remaining cookies, frosting and licorice.

9 Attach snack cake to 1 end of worm using frosting.

10 Decorate with cookies and assorted candies to resemble face.

Makes 1 worm (3 dozen cookies)

Tip

To make this party worm into a cute birthday worm, insert birthday candles into the frosting used to hold the cookies together. It's sure to be the hit of the party.

Cookie Pizza

What you need:

1 package (20 ounces) refrigerated sugar or peanut butter cookie dough
All-purpose flour (optional)
6 ounces (1 cup) semisweet chocolate chips
1 tablespoon plus 2 teaspoons shortening, divided
¼ cup white chocolate chips

TOPPINGS

Gummy fruit, chocolate-covered peanuts, assorted roasted nuts, raisins, jelly beans and other assorted candies

1 Preheat oven to 350°F. Generously grease 12-inch pizza pan.

2 Remove dough from wrapper according to package directions.

3 Sprinkle dough with flour to minimize sticking, if necessary. Press dough into bottom of prepared pan, leaving about ¾-inch space between edge of dough and pan.

4 Bake 14 to 23 minutes or until golden brown and set in center. Cool completely in pan on wire rack, running spatula between cookie crust and pan after 10 to 15 minutes to loosen.

5 Melt semisweet chocolate chips and 1 tablespoon shortening in microwavable bowl at HIGH (100%) 1 minute; stir. Repeat process at 10 to 20 second intervals until smooth.

6 Melt white chocolate chips and remaining 2 teaspoons shortening in another microwavable bowl at MEDIUM-HIGH (70%) 1 minute; stir. Repeat process at 10 to 20 second intervals until smooth.

7 Spread melted semisweet chocolate mixture over crust to within 1 inch of edge. Decorate with desired toppings.

8 Drizzle melted white chocolate over toppings to resemble melted mozzarella cheese. Cut and serve.

Makes 10 to 12 pizza slices

Name Jewelry

What you need:

1 recipe Christmas Ornament Cookie Dough (page 159)

SUPPLIES

Plastic drinking straw
Thin ribbon or yarn

DECORATIONS

White Icing (recipe follows)
Colored sugars
Assorted food colors (optional)
Small candies (optional)

1 Prepare Christmas Ornament Cookie Dough. Divide dough in half; wrap in plastic wrap. Refrigerate 30 minutes or until firm.

2 Preheat oven to 350°F. Grease cookie sheets.

3 Roll ½ of dough on floured surface to ¼-inch thickness. Cut out cookies using 3¾-inch cookie cutters of various shapes, such as rectangles, circles and hearts.

4 Place cookies on prepared cookie sheets. With plastic straw, make holes in tops of cookies, about ½ inch from top edges.

5 Bake 10 to 12 minutes or until edges begin to brown. Remove cookies to wire racks; cool completely. If necessary, push straw through warm cookies to remake holes.

6 Cut ribbon into 18 (32-inch) pieces. Thread ribbon through holes.

7 Prepare White Icing; spread over cookies. Let stand 40 minutes or until set. Spoon colored or additional icing into small resealable plastic food storage bag. Cut tiny tip from corner of bag. Pipe individual names directly onto cookies as shown in photo. Let stand until set. Decorate with colored sugars and small candies, if desired.

Makes about 18 cookie necklaces

White Icing

2 cups powdered sugar
2 tablespoons milk or lemon juice

Combine powdered sugar and milk in small bowl until smooth. (Icing will be very thick. Stir in 1 teaspoon additional milk, if desired.) Icing may be divided into small bowls and tinted with food coloring, if desired.

Emily
LAUREN

Sunshine Butter Cookies

What you need:

¾ cup butter, softened
¾ cup sugar
1 egg
2¼ cups all-purpose flour
¼ teaspoon salt
Grated peel of ½ lemon
1 teaspoon frozen lemonade concentrate, thawed
1 recipe Lemonade Royal Icing (page 160)
1 egg, beaten
Thin pretzel sticks
Yellow paste food color

DECORATIONS

Gummy fruit and black licorice strings

1 Beat butter and sugar in large bowl at high speed of electric mixer until fluffy. Add egg; beat well.

2 Combine flour, salt and lemon peel in medium bowl. Add to butter mixture. Stir in lemonade concentrate. Refrigerate 2 hours.

3 Prepare Lemonade Royal Icing. Cover; let stand at room temperature. Preheat oven to 350°F. Grease cookie sheets.

4 Roll dough on floured surface to ⅛-inch thickness. Cut out cookies using 3-inch round cookie cutter. Place cookies on prepared cookie sheets. Brush cookies with beaten egg. Arrange pretzel sticks around edge of cookies to resemble sunshine rays; press gently. Bake 10 minutes or until lightly browned. Remove to wire racks; cool completely.

5 Add food color to Lemonade Royal Icing. Spoon about ½ cup icing into resealable plastic food storage bag; seal. Cut tiny tip from corner of bag. Pipe thin circle around underside of each cookie to create outline.

6 Add water, 1 tablespoon at a time, to remaining icing in bowl, until thick but pourable consistency. Spoon icing in cookie centers staying within outline.

7 Decorate cookies with fruit snacks and licorice as shown in photo. Let stand 1 hour or until dry.

Makes about 3 dozen cookies

Chocolate Pinwheels

What you need:

1 recipe Chocolate Cookie Dough (page 158)

SUPPLIES

24 wooden popsicle sticks

DECORATIONS

24 (¼-inch) round hard candies or other candies

Assorted colored sugars

1 Prepare Chocolate Cookie Dough. Cover; refrigerate 1 hour or until firm.

2 Preheat oven to 325°F. Grease cookie sheets. Place popsicle sticks 4 inches apart on prepared cookie sheets.

3 Roll dough on floured surface to ¼-inch thickness. Cut out cookies using 3-inch round cookie cutter.

4 Place 1 dough round on end of each wooden stick, pressing down. Cut 4 (1-inch) slits around the edge of each dough round according to diagram.

5 Lift 1 side of each slit, bringing the corner to the center of the cookie and pressing gently. Repeat with remaining dough. Place round candy in center of each pinwheel cookie.

6 Bake 10 minutes or until set. Remove to wire racks; cool completely. Decorate with colored sugars.

Makes 2 dozen cookies

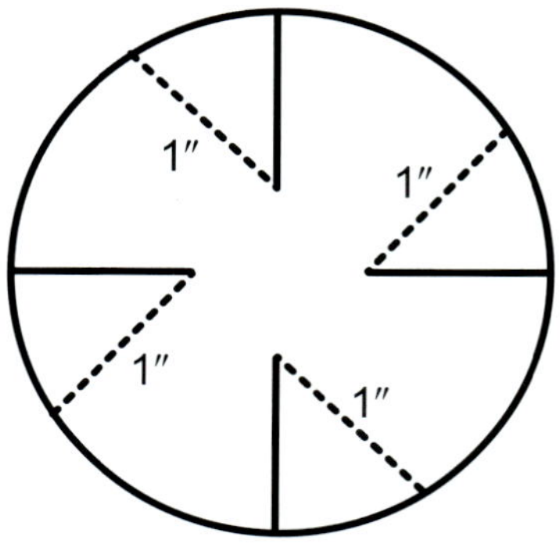

3″ circle

Holiday Treats

Festive Easter Cookies

What you need:

1 cup butter, softened
2 cups powdered sugar
1 egg
2 teaspoons grated lemon peel
1 teaspoon vanilla
3 cups all-purpose flour
½ teaspoon salt
1 recipe Royal Icing (page 160)

DECORATIONS
Assorted food colors, icings and candies

1 Beat butter and sugar in large bowl at high speed of electric mixer until fluffy. Add egg, lemon peel and vanilla; mix well. Combine flour and salt in medium bowl. Add to butter mixture; mix well.

2 Divide dough into 2 sections. Cover with plastic wrap. Refrigerate 3 hours or overnight.

3 Preheat oven to 375°F. Roll dough on floured surface to ⅛-inch thickness. Cut out cookies using Easter cookie cutters, such as eggs, bunnies and tulips. Place on ungreased cookie sheets.

4 Bake 8 to 12 minutes or just until edges are very lightly browned. Remove to wire racks; cool completely. Prepare Royal Icing. Decorate as desired. Let stand until icing is set.

Makes 4 dozen cookies

Festive Easter Cookies

Chocolate and Peanut Butter Hearts

What you need:

- **1 recipe Chocolate Cookie Dough (page 158)**
- **½ cup creamy peanut butter**
- **½ cup shortening**
- **1 cup sugar**
- **1 egg**
- **1 teaspoon vanilla**
- **3 tablespoons milk**
- **2 cups all-purpose flour**
- **1 teaspoon baking powder**
- **¼ teaspoon salt**

1 Prepare Chocolate Cookie Dough. Divide dough in half; wrap in plastic wrap. Refrigerate about 2 hours or until firm.

2 Beat peanut butter, shortening and sugar at medium speed of electric mixer until fluffy. Add egg and vanilla; mix until well blended. Add milk; mix well.

3 Combine flour, baking powder and salt in medium bowl. Add flour mixture to peanut butter mixture; mix at low speed until well blended. Divide dough in half; wrap in plastic wrap. Refrigerate 1 to 2 hours or until firm.

4 Preheat oven to 350°F. Grease cookie sheets. Roll ½ of peanut butter dough on floured waxed paper to ⅛-inch thickness. Cut out cookies using 3-inch heart-shaped cookie cutter. Place on prepared cookie sheets.

5 Use smaller heart-shaped cookie cutter to remove small section from center of heart; set smaller cutouts aside.

6 Repeat with chocolate dough. Place small hearts into opposite dough according to photo; press lightly.

7 Bake 12 to 14 minutes or until edges are lightly browned. Remove to wire racks; cool completely.

Makes 4 dozen cookies

To my Valentine

Angels

What you need:

1 recipe Butter Cookie Dough (page 158)
1 egg, lightly beaten

DECORATIONS

Small pretzels, white frosting, toasted coconut, glitter dust and assorted small decors

1 Prepare Butter Cookie Dough. Refrigerate about 6 hours or until firm.

2 Preheat oven to 350°F. Grease cookie sheets. Roll dough on floured surface to ¼-inch thickness.

3 Cut out 12 (4-inch) triangles according to diagram. Reroll scraps to ¼-inch thickness. Cut out 12 (1½-inch) circles according to diagram.

4 Place triangles on prepared cookie sheets. Brush tops with beaten egg. Attach circle, pressing gently.

5 Bake 8 to 10 minutes or just until edges begin to brown. Remove to wire racks; cool completely.

6 Attach pretzels to back of each cookie for wings using frosting as "glue". Let dry 30 minutes. Pipe frosting around hairline of each angel; sprinkle with coconut and glitter dust.

7 Pipe frosting on body of cookie to resemble arms and gown. Decorate faces as desired. Let stand 1 hour or until dry.

Makes 1 dozen cookies

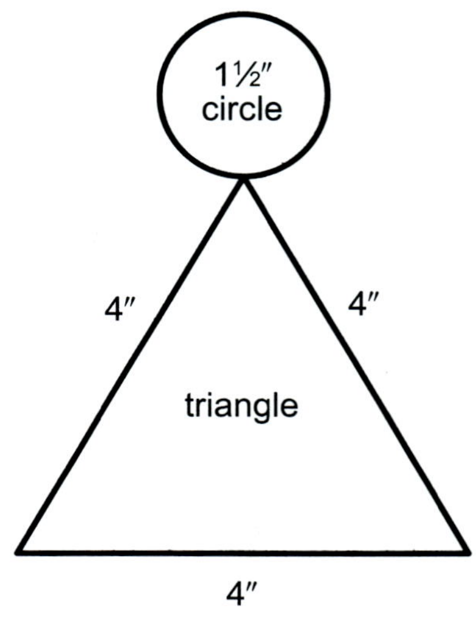

Christmas Tree Platter

What you need:

1 recipe Christmas Ornament Cookie Dough (page 159)
2 cups sifted powdered sugar
2 tablespoons milk or lemon juice

DECORATIONS

Assorted food colors, colored sugars and assorted small decors

1 Preheat oven to 350°F. Prepare Christmas Ornament Cookie Dough. Divide dough in half. Reserve 1 half; refrigerate remaining dough. Roll reserved half of dough to ⅛-inch thickness.

2 Cut out tree shapes with cookie cutters. Place on ungreased cookie sheets.

3 Bake 10 to 12 minutes or until edges are lightly browned. Remove to wire racks; cool completely.

4 Repeat with remaining half of dough. Reroll scraps; cut into small circles for ornaments, squares and rectangles for gift boxes and tree trunks.

5 Bake 8 to 12 minutes, depending on size of cookies.

6 Mix sugar and milk for icing. Tint most of icing green and a smaller amount red or other colors for ornaments and boxes. Spread green icing on trees. Sprinkle ornaments and boxes with colored sugars or decorate as desired.

7 Arrange cookies on flat platter to resemble tree as shown in photo.

Makes about 1 dozen cookies

Tip

Use this beautiful Christmas Tree Platter cookie as your centerpiece for this holiday's family dinner. It's sure to receive lots of "oohs" and "ahs"!

Snowmen

What you need:

1 package (20 ounces) refrigerated chocolate chip cookie dough
1½ cups sifted powdered sugar
2 tablespoons milk

DECORATIONS
Candy corn, gum drops, chocolate chips, licorice and other assorted small candies

1 Preheat oven to 375°F.

2 Cut dough into 12 equal sections. Divide each section into 3 balls: large, medium and small for each snowman.

3 For each snowman, place 3 balls in a row, ¼ inch apart, on ungreased cookie sheet. Repeat with remaining dough.

4 Bake 10 to 12 minutes or until edges are very lightly browned.

5 Cool 4 minutes on cookie sheets. Remove to wire racks; cool completely.

6 Mix powdered sugar and milk in medium bowl until smooth. Pour over cookies. Let cookies stand 20 minutes or until set.

7 Decorate to create faces, hats and arms with assorted candies.

Makes 1 dozen cookies

Tip

Create your own holiday village by baking several batches of Snowmen, Angels (page 148) and 1 Gingerbread Log Cabin (page 154).

Gingerbread Log Cabin

What you need:

7 cups all-purpose flour
1 tablespoon plus 1½ teaspoons ground ginger
2¾ teaspoons baking soda
2¼ teaspoons ground allspice
1¼ teaspoons salt
2⅔ cups packed brown sugar
1⅓ cups butter, softened
1 cup dark corn syrup
3 eggs

SUPPLIES

Cardboard
Aluminum foil

DECORATIONS

Royal Icing (page 160)
Assorted food colors
Assorted gum drops and hard candies

1 Draw patterns for house on cardboard, using diagrams on page 156; cut out patterns. Preheat oven to 375°F. Grease and flour large cookie sheet. Combine flour, ginger, baking soda, allspice and salt in medium bowl.

2 Beat brown sugar and butter in large bowl at medium speed of electric mixer until fluffy. Beat in corn syrup and eggs. Gradually add 6 cups flour mixture to brown sugar mixture. Beat until well blended. Stir in remaining flour mixture with wooden spoon. Divide dough into 4 equal sections. Reserve 1 section; refrigerate remaining 3 sections.

3 To make sides of cabin, roll reserved dough directly onto prepared cookie sheet to ¼-inch thickness. Lay sheet of waxed paper over dough. Place patterns over waxed paper 2 inches apart. Cut dough around pattern with sharp knife; remove patterns and waxed paper. Reserve scraps to reroll with next section of dough.

4 To make logs, roll dough into 12 (1-inch) balls. Roll each ball into 6-inch rope. Lay 6 logs parallel to one another on 1 prepared house side, leaving ¼-inch border at top and bottom of house side. Repeat steps with remaining 6 balls and second side. Freeze 15 minutes.

5 Bake 15 to 18 minutes or until no indentation remains when cookies are touched in center. While cookies are still hot, place cardboard pattern lightly over cookies; trim edges with sharp knife to straighten. Return to oven 2 minutes. Let stand on cookie sheets 5 minutes. Remove using spatula

continued on page 156

Gingerbread Log Cabin, continued

to wire racks; cool completely. Leave cookie pieces out uncovered overnight.

6 To make front and back walls, repeat step 3. To make logs for front and back, roll dough into 18 (1¼-inch) balls. Roll each ball into 7-inch log. Place 9 logs for front wall over cardboard pattern as a guide; cut out openings for windows. Lay logs parallel on front wall, leaving ¼-inch border at top and bottom of wall. Repeat steps with remaining 9 balls and back wall. Freeze 15 minutes. Bake and reserve as directed in step 5.

7 To make roof, repeat step 3. To make logs for roof, roll dough into 16 (1¼-inch) balls. Roll each ball into 7½-inch log. Lay logs parallel to one another on roof, leaving ¼-inch border at top and bottom of roof. Freeze 15 minutes. Bake and reserve as directed in step 5.

8 To make chimney, roll cookie scraps into ball. Roll and cut out rectangle about 3×1¾-inches. Bake 10 to 12 minutes.

9 Cover 15-inch square piece of heavy cardboard with foil to use as base for cabin. Prepare Royal Icing. Place icing in small resealable plastic food storage bag. Cut off small corner of bag. Pipe icing on edges of all pieces including bottom; "glue" house together at seams and on base.

10 Position mug against outside of each wall and another at inside corner where 2 walls meet. Let dry at least 6 hours. When icing is set, remove mugs from inside walls. Pipe icing onto roof edges and attach to house. Place mug under each side of roof. Let dry at least 6 hours. Decorate with additional icing and candies as desired. Place chimney near top of one side of roof; attach with icing.

11 Pipe icing on cabin to resemble snow. Decorate as desired.

Makes 1 gingerbread log cabin

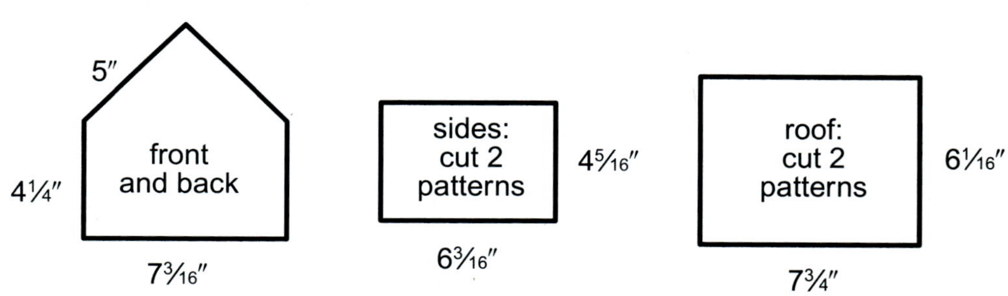

Basic Recipes

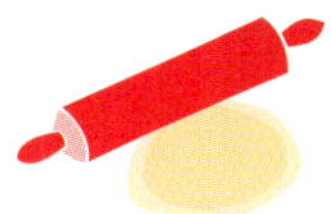

Yield and baking times have not been included for these cookies. For best results, prepare and bake as directed in individual recipes.

Gingerbread Cookie Dough

What you need:

½ cup shortening
⅓ cup packed light brown sugar
¼ cup dark molasses
1 egg white
½ teaspoon vanilla
1½ cups all-purpose flour
1 teaspoon ground cinnamon
½ teaspoon baking soda
½ teaspoon salt
½ teaspoon ground ginger
¼ teaspoon baking powder

1 Beat shortening, brown sugar, molasses, egg white and vanilla in large bowl at high speed of electric mixer until smooth.

2 Combine flour, cinnamon, baking soda, salt, ginger and baking powder in small bowl. Add to shortening mixture; mix well. Cover; refrigerate about 8 hours or until firm.

Butter Cookie Dough

What you need:

¾ cup butter, softened
¼ cup granulated sugar
¼ cup packed light brown sugar
1 egg yolk
1¾ cups all-purpose flour
¾ teaspoon baking powder
⅛ teaspoon salt

1 Combine butter, granulated sugar, brown sugar and egg yolk in medium bowl. Add flour, baking powder and salt; mix well.

2 Cover; refrigerate about 4 hours or until firm.

Chocolate Cookie Dough

What you need:

1 cup butter, softened
1 cup sugar
1 egg
1 teaspoon vanilla
2 ounces semisweet chocolate, melted
2¼ cups all-purpose flour
1 teaspoon baking powder
¼ teaspoon salt

1 Beat butter and sugar in large bowl at high speed of electric mixer until fluffy. Beat in egg and vanilla. Add melted chocolate; mix well.

2 Add flour, baking powder and salt; mix well. Cover; refrigerate about 2 hours or until firm.

Christmas Ornament Cookie Dough

What you need:

2¼ cups all-purpose flour
¼ teaspoon salt
1 cup sugar
¾ cup butter, softened
1 egg
1 teaspoon vanilla
1 teaspoon almond extract

1 Combine flour and salt in medium bowl.

2 Beat sugar and butter in large bowl at medium speed of electric mixer until fluffy. Beat in egg, vanilla and almond extract. Gradually add flour mixture. Beat at low speed until well blended.

3 Form dough into 2 discs; wrap in plastic wrap and refrigerate 30 minutes or until firm.

Gingerbread House Dough

What you need:

5¼ cups all-purpose flour
1 tablespoon ground ginger
2 teaspoons baking soda
1½ teaspoons ground allspice
1 teaspoon salt
2 cups packed dark brown sugar
1 cup butter, softened
¾ cup dark corn syrup
2 eggs

1 Combine flour, ginger, baking soda, allspice and salt in medium bowl.

2 Beat brown sugar and butter in large bowl at medium speed of electric mixer until fluffy. Beat in corn syrup and eggs. Gradually add flour mixture. Beat at low speed until well blended. Cover; refrigerate about 2 hours or until firm.

Royal Icing

What you need:

1 egg white, at room temperature
2 to 2½ cups sifted powdered sugar
½ teaspoon almond extract

1 Beat egg white in small bowl at high speed of electric mixer until foamy.

2 Gradually add 2 cups powdered sugar and almond extract. Beat at low speed until moistened. Increase mixer speed to high and beat until icing is stiff.

Lemonade Royal Icing

What you need:

3¾ cups sifted powdered sugar
3 tablespoons meringue powder
6 tablespoons frozen lemonade concentrate, thawed

Beat all ingredients in large bowl at high speed of electric mixer until smooth.

Cookie Glaze

What you need:

4 cups powdered sugar
4 to 6 tablespoons milk

Combine powdered sugar and enough milk, 1 tablespoon at a time, to make a medium-thick pourable glaze.

Contents

Rise and shine! Nothing gets kids moving in the morning like a hearty breakfast. Add a fun twist to the A.M. with these waffles, pancakes and other tasty sunrise specials.

Chocolate Chip Waffles

- 1 package DUNCAN HINES® Chocolate Chip Muffin Mix
- ¾ cup all-purpose flour
- 1 teaspoon baking powder
- 1¾ cups milk
- 2 eggs
- 5 tablespoons butter or margarine, melted
- Confectioners' sugar (optional)

Preheat and lightly grease waffle iron according to manufacturer's directions.

Combine muffin mix, flour and baking powder in large bowl. Add milk, eggs and melted butter. Stir until moistened, about 50 strokes. Pour batter onto center grids of preheated waffle iron. Bake according to manufacturer's directions until golden brown. Remove baked waffle carefully with fork. Repeat with remaining batter. Dust lightly with sugar, if desired. Top with fresh fruit, syrup, grated chocolate or whipped cream, if desired.

Makes 10 to 12 waffles

Chocolate Chip Waffles

Breakfast Pizza

1 can (10 ounces) refrigerated biscuit dough
½ pound bacon slices
2 tablespoons butter or margarine
2 tablespoons all-purpose flour
¼ teaspoon salt
⅛ teaspoon black pepper
1½ cups milk
½ cup (2 ounces) shredded sharp Cheddar cheese
¼ cup sliced green onions
¼ cup chopped red bell pepper

Preheat oven to 350°F. Spray 13×9-inch baking dish with nonstick cooking spray.

Separate biscuit dough and arrange in rectangle on lightly floured surface. Roll into 14×10-inch rectangle. Place in prepared dish; pat edges up sides of dish. Bake 15 minutes. Remove from oven and set aside.

Meanwhile, place bacon in single layer in large skillet; cook over medium heat until crisp. Remove from skillet; drain on paper towels. Crumble and set aside.

Melt butter in medium saucepan over medium heat. Stir in flour, salt and black pepper until smooth. Gradually stir in milk; cook and stir until thickened. Stir in cheese until melted. Spread sauce evenly over baked crust. Arrange bacon, green onions and bell pepper over sauce.

Bake, uncovered, 20 minutes or until crust is golden brown.

Makes 6 servings

Breakfast Pizza

Bunny Pancakes with Strawberry Butter

- Strawberry Butter (recipe follows)
- 2 cups buttermilk baking mix
- 1 cup milk
- 2 eggs
- ½ cup plain yogurt
- Assorted candies

1. Prepare Strawberry Butter; set aside. Preheat electric skillet or griddle to 375°F.

2. Combine baking mix, milk, eggs and yogurt in medium bowl; mix well. Spoon scant ½ cup batter into skillet. With back of spoon, gently spread batter into 4-inch circle. Spoon about 2 tablespoons batter onto top edge of circle for head. Using back of spoon, spread batter from head to form bunny ears as shown in photo.

3. Cook until bubbles on surface begin to pop and top of pancake appears dry; turn pancake over. Cook until done, 1 to 2 minutes. Decorate with candies as shown in photo.

4. Repeat with remaining batter. Serve warm with Strawberry Butter.

Makes about 12 (8-inch) pancakes

Strawberry Butter: Place 1 package (3 ounces) cream cheese and ½ cup softened butter in food processor or blender; process until smooth. Add ⅓ cup sugar; process until combined. Add 1½ cups fresh or thawed frozen strawberries; process until finely chopped.

Reindeer Pancakes: Prepare batter as directed. Spoon scant ¼ cup batter into skillet. Quickly spread batter with back of spoon to form antlers as shown in photo. Cook as directed. Decorate as shown in photo. Serve as directed.

Top to bottom: Reindeer Pancake, Bunny Pancake with Strawberry Butter

Peanut Butter & Banana Wake-up Shake

1 cup (8 ounces) vanilla yogurt
1 cup milk
1/3 cup SKIPPY® Creamy Peanut Butter
1/4 cup KARO® Light or Dark Corn Syrup
1 ripe banana, cut into chunks
5 ice cubes

1. In blender combine yogurt, milk, peanut butter, corn syrup and banana; process until smooth.

2. With blender running, gradually add ice cubes. Blend until thickened and smooth. Serve immediately.

Makes about 4 (8-ounce) servings

Prep Time: 5 minutes

Breakfast Blossoms

1 (12-ounce) can buttermilk biscuits (10 biscuits)
3/4 cup SMUCKER'S® Strawberry Preserves
1/4 teaspoon ground cinnamon
1/4 teaspoon ground nutmeg

Grease ten 2½- or 3-inch muffin cups. Separate dough into 10 biscuits. Separate each biscuit into 3 even sections or leaves. Stand 3 sections evenly around sides and bottom of cup, overlapping slightly. Press dough edges firmly together.

Combine preserves, cinnamon and nutmeg; place scant tablespoonful in center of each cup.

Bake at 375°F for 10 to 12 minutes or until lightly browned. Cool slightly before removing from pan. Serve warm. *Makes 10 rolls*

French Toast Sticks

1 cup EGG BEATERS® Healthy Real Egg Product
⅓ cup skim milk
1 teaspoon ground cinnamon
1 teaspoon vanilla extract
2 tablespoons FLEISCHMANN'S® Original Margarine, divided
16 (4×1×1-inch) sticks day-old white bread
Powdered sugar, optional
Maple-flavored syrup, optional

In shallow bowl, combine Egg Beaters®, milk, cinnamon and vanilla.

In large nonstick griddle or skillet, over medium-high heat, melt 2 teaspoons margarine. Dip bread sticks in egg mixture to coat; transfer to griddle. Cook sticks on each side until golden, adding remaining margarine as needed. Dust lightly with powdered sugar and serve with syrup, if desired.

Makes 4 servings

Prep Time: 15 minutes
Cook Time: 18 minutes

Breakfast Baskets

8 (6-inch) flour tortillas, divided
4 tablespoons butter, melted and divided
4 bacon slices, cut into 1-inch pieces
½ cup chopped green bell pepper
½ cup chopped red bell pepper
3 tablespoons chopped onion
4 eggs
3 tablespoons milk
¼ teaspoon salt
¼ teaspoon hot pepper sauce (optional)
⅛ teaspoon black pepper

1. Preheat oven to 350°F.

2. Brush 6 tortillas with melted butter; let stand until pliable, about 5 minutes. Gently ease buttered tortillas into 6 small custard cups.

3. For handles, cut each of both remaining tortillas into 3 (1-inch) strips. (There should be 6 strips.) Brush with remaining butter. Invert muffin pan; arrange 2 strips in "u" shape around bottoms of each of 3 cups. Bake tortilla cups and handles 10 to 15 minutes or until golden brown. Remove cups and handles to wire rack; cool.

4. Meanwhile, cook bacon in medium skillet over medium-high heat until crisp, stirring occasionally. Remove bacon from skillet; set aside. Pour off all but 1 tablespoon bacon fat from skillet. Add bell peppers and onion to skillet; cook and stir until crisp-tender.

5. Whisk together eggs, milk, salt, hot pepper sauce and pepper. Add to vegetable mixture in skillet; cook and stir until eggs are set. Stir in bacon. Divide egg mixture evenly among prepared baskets. Place handles in baskets. Serve warm. *Makes 6 servings*

Breakfast Baskets

Cinnamon-Raisin Rolls

1 package (16 ounces) hot roll mix plus ingredients to prepare mix
⅓ cup raisins
4 tablespoons butter, softened and divided
¼ cup granulated sugar
2 teaspoons ground cinnamon
½ teaspoon ground nutmeg
1½ cups powdered sugar
1 to 2 tablespoons fat-free (skim) milk
½ teaspoon vanilla

1. Preheat oven to 375°F. Spray 13×9-inch baking pan with nonstick cooking spray.

2. Prepare hot roll mix according to package directions; mix in raisins. Knead dough on lightly floured surface until smooth and elastic, about 5 minutes. Cover dough with plastic wrap; let stand 5 minutes.

3. Roll out dough on floured surface to 16×10-inch rectangle. Spread dough with 2 tablespoons butter. Combine granulated sugar, cinnamon and nutmeg in small bowl; sprinkle evenly over dough. Roll up dough starting at long end. Pinch edge of dough to seal.

4. Gently stretch sealed dough until 18 inches long. Cut dough into 1-inch pieces; place, cut side up, in prepared pan. Cover pan loosely with towel. Let stand 20 to 30 minutes or until doubled in size.

5. Bake 20 to 25 minutes or until golden. Cool in pan on wire rack 2 to 3 minutes. Remove from pan; cool on wire rack.

6. Combine powdered sugar, remaining 2 tablespoons butter, 1 tablespoon milk and vanilla in medium bowl. Add additional 1 tablespoon milk to make thin glaze, if desired. Spread glaze over warm rolls.

Makes 1½ dozen rolls

Cinnamon-Raisin Rolls

Move over, milk and cookies! Your kids will gobble up these fun and filling munchies. Refuel empty tummies with smoothies, snack mixes, dips and much more.

Pizza Snack Cups

- 1 can (12 ounces) refrigerated biscuits (10 biscuits)
- ½ pound ground beef
- 1 jar (14 ounces) RAGÚ® Pizza Quick® Sauce
- ½ cup shredded mozzarella cheese (about 2 ounces)

1. Preheat oven to 375°F. In 12-cup muffin pan, evenly press each biscuit in bottom and up side of each cup; chill until ready to fill.
2. In 10-inch skillet, brown ground beef over medium-high heat; drain. Stir in Ragú Pizza Quick Sauce and heat through.
3. Evenly spoon beef mixture into prepared muffin cups. Bake 15 minutes. Sprinkle with cheese and bake an additional 5 minutes or until cheese is melted and biscuits are golden. Let stand 5 minutes. Gently remove pizza cups from muffin pan and serve. *Makes 10 pizza cups*

Prep Time: 10 minutes
Cook Time: 25 minutes

Pizza Snack Cups

Super Nachos

12 large baked low-fat tortilla chips (about 1½ ounces)
½ cup (2 ounces) shredded reduced-fat Cheddar cheese
¼ cup fat-free refried beans
2 tablespoons chunky salsa

1. Arrange chips in single layer on large microwavable plate. Sprinkle cheese evenly over chips.

2. Spoon beans over chips; top with salsa.

3. Microwave at MEDIUM (50%) 1½ minutes; rotate dish. Microwave 1 to 1½ minutes or until cheese is melted.

Makes 2 servings

Conventional Directions: Substitute foil-covered baking sheet for microwavable plate. Assemble nachos as directed on prepared baking sheet. Bake at 350°F 10 to 12 minutes or until cheese is melted.

Cook's Tip: For a single serving of nachos, arrange 6 large tortilla chips on microwavable plate; top with ¼ cup cheese, 2 tablespoons beans and 1 tablespoon salsa. Microwave at MEDIUM (50%) 1 minute; rotate dish. Continue to microwave 30 seconds to 1 minute or until cheese is melted.

Super Nachos

Honey Popcorn Clusters

Vegetable cooking spray
6 cups air-popped popcorn
⅔ cup DOLE® Golden or Seedless Raisins
½ cup DOLE® Chopped Dates or Pitted Dates, chopped
⅓ cup DOLE® Slivered Almonds (optional)
⅓ cup packed brown sugar
¼ cup honey
2 tablespoons margarine
¼ teaspoon baking soda

• Line bottom and sides of 13×9-inch baking pan with large sheet of aluminum foil. Spray foil with vegetable cooking spray.

• Stir together popcorn, raisins, dates and almonds in foil-lined pan.

• Combine brown sugar, honey and margarine in small saucepan. Bring to boil over medium heat, stirring constantly; reduce heat to low. Cook 5 minutes. *Do not stir.* Remove from heat.

• Stir in baking soda. Pour evenly over popcorn mixture, stirring quickly to coat mixture evenly.

• Bake at 300°F 12 to 15 minutes or until mixture is lightly browned, stirring once halfway through baking time.

• Lift foil from pan; place on cooling rack. Cool popcorn mixture completely; break into clusters. Popcorn can be stored in airtight container up to 1 week. *Makes 7 cups*

Prep Time: 20 minutes
Bake Time: 15 minutes

Pepperoni Pizza Dip

1 cup RAGÚ® Old World Style® Pasta Sauce
1 cup RAGÚ® Cheese Creations!® Classic Alfredo Sauce
1 cup shredded mozzarella cheese (about 4 ounces)
¼ to ½ cup finely chopped pepperoni

1. In 2-quart saucepan, heat Ragú Pasta Sauces, cheese and pepperoni, stirring occasionally, 10 minutes or until cheese is melted.

2. Pour into 1½-quart casserole or serving dish and serve, if desired, with breadsticks, sliced Italian bread or crackers.

Makes 3½ cups dip

Prep Time: 5 minutes
Cook Time: 10 minutes

Philadelphia® Fruit Dip

1 package (8 ounces) PHILADELPHIA® Cream Cheese, softened
1 container (8 ounces) strawberry or any flavored yogurt

MIX cream cheese and yogurt with electric mixer on medium speed until well blended. Refrigerate.

SERVE with assorted fresh fruit. *Makes about 1⅔ cups*

Prep Time: 5 minutes plus refrigerating

Super Spread Sandwich Stars

- 1 Red or Golden Delicious apple, peeled, cored and coarsely chopped
- 1 cup roasted peanuts
- ⅓ cup honey
- 1 tablespoon lemon juice
- 1 teaspoon ground cinnamon
- Sliced sandwich bread

For Super Spread, place chopped apple, peanuts, honey, lemon juice and cinnamon in food processor or blender. Pulse food processor several times until ingredients start to blend, occasionally scraping down the sides with rubber spatula. Process 1 to 2 minutes until mixture is smooth and spreadable.

For Sandwich Stars, use butter knife to spread about 1 tablespoon Super Spread on 2 slices of bread. Stack them together, spread side up. Top with third slice bread. Place cookie cutter on top of sandwich; press down firmly and evenly. Leaving cookie cutter in place, remove excess trimmings with your fingers or a butter knife. Remove cookie cutter.

Makes 1¼ cups spread (enough for about 10 sandwiches)

Favorite recipe from **Texas Peanut Producers Board**

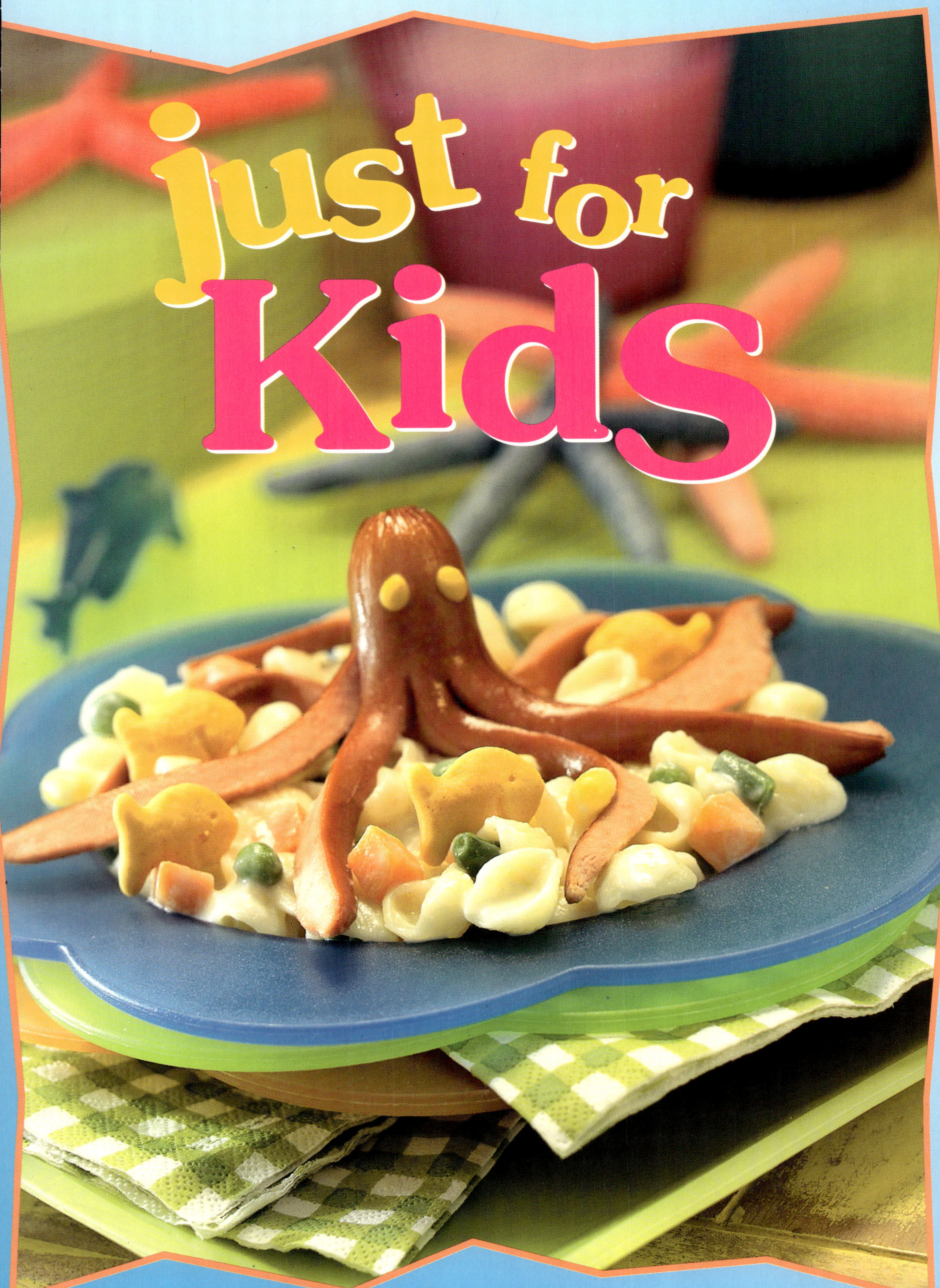
just for
Kids

Super Spread Sandwich Stars

Creamy Taco Dip

1 pound (16 ounces) VELVEETA® Pasteurized Prepared Cheese Product, cut up
1 container (16 ounces) BREAKSTONE'S® or KNUDSEN® Sour Cream
1 package (1¼ ounces) TACO BELL® HOME ORIGINALS™ Taco Seasoning Mix

Microwave all ingredients in 2-quart microwavable bowl on HIGH 5 minutes or until Velveeta is melted, stirring after 3 minutes. Serve hot or cold with corn chips or tortilla chips. *Makes 3½ cups*

Prep Time: 5 minutes
Microwave Time: 5 minutes

Tuna 'n' Celery Sticks

4 ounces cream cheese, softened
3 tablespoons plain yogurt or mayonnaise
1½ teaspoons dried basil
1 can (12 ounces) STARKIST® Solid White or Chunk Light Tuna, drained and flaked
½ cup finely grated carrot or zucchini
½ cup finely shredded Cheddar cheese
2 teaspoons instant minced onion
10 to 12 celery stalks, cleaned and strings removed

In large bowl, mix together cream cheese, yogurt and basil until smooth. Add tuna, carrot, Cheddar cheese and onion; mix well. Spread mixture into celery stalks; cut into fourths.

Makes 40 servings

Prep Time: 10 minutes

Creamy Taco Dip

Inside-Out Turkey Sandwiches

2 tablespoons cream cheese
2 tablespoons pasteurized process cheese spread
2 teaspoons chopped green onion tops
1 teaspoon prepared mustard
12 thin round slices turkey breast or smoked turkey breast
4 large pretzel logs or unsalted breadsticks

1. Combine cream cheese, process cheese spread, green onion and mustard in small bowl; mix well.

2. Arrange 3 turkey slices on large sheet of plastic wrap, overlapping slices in center. Spread ¼ of cream cheese mixture evenly onto turkey slices, covering slices completely. Place 1 pretzel at bottom edge of turkey slices; roll up turkey around pretzel. (Be sure to keep all 3 turkey slices together as you roll them around pretzel.)

3. Repeat with remaining ingredients. *Makes 4 servings*

Original Ranch® Snack Mix

8 cups Kellogg's® Crispix® cereal
2½ cups small pretzels
2½ cups bite-size Cheddar cheese crackers (optional)
3 tablespoons vegetable oil
1 packet (1 ounce) Hidden Valley® Original Ranch® Dressing Mix

Combine cereal, pretzels and crackers in large plastic bag. Pour oil over mixture and toss to coat. Add dressing mix; toss again until coated. *Makes about 10 cups*

Inside-Out Turkey Sandwiches

Frozen Chocolate-Covered Bananas

2 ripe medium bananas
4 wooden sticks
½ cup low-fat granola cereal without raisins
⅓ cup hot fudge sauce, at room temperature

1. Cover baking sheet or 15×10-inch jelly-roll pan with waxed paper; set aside.

2. Peel bananas; cut each in half crosswise. Insert wooden stick into center of cut end of each banana about 1½ inches into banana half. Place on prepared baking sheet; freeze until firm, at least 2 hours.

3. Place granola in large plastic food storage bag; crush slightly using rolling pin or meat mallet. Transfer granola to shallow plate. Place fudge sauce in a shallow dish.

4. Working with 1 banana at a time, place frozen banana in fudge sauce; turn banana and spread fudge sauce evenly onto banana with small rubber scraper. Immediately place banana on plate with granola; turn to coat lightly. Return to baking sheet in freezer. Repeat with remaining bananas.

5. Freeze until fudge sauce is very firm, at least 2 hours. Place on small plates; let stand 5 minutes before serving. *Makes 4 servings*

Berry Striped Pops

- 2 cups strawberries
- 3/4 cup honey,* divided
- 6 kiwifruit, peeled and sliced
- 2 cups sliced peaches
- 12 (3-ounce) paper cups or popsicle molds
- 12 popsicle sticks

**Honey should not be fed to infants under one year of age. Honey is a safe and wholesome food for older children and adults.*

Purée strawberries with 1/4 cup honey in blender or food processor. Divide mixture evenly between 12 cups or popsicle molds. Freeze about 30 minutes or until firm. Meanwhile, rinse processor; purée kiwifruit with 1/4 cup honey. Repeat process with peaches and remaining 1/4 cup honey. When strawberry layer is firm, pour kiwifruit purée into molds. Insert popsicle sticks and freeze about 30 minutes or until firm. Pour peach purée into molds and freeze until firm and ready to serve.

Makes 12 servings

Favorite recipe from **National Honey Board**

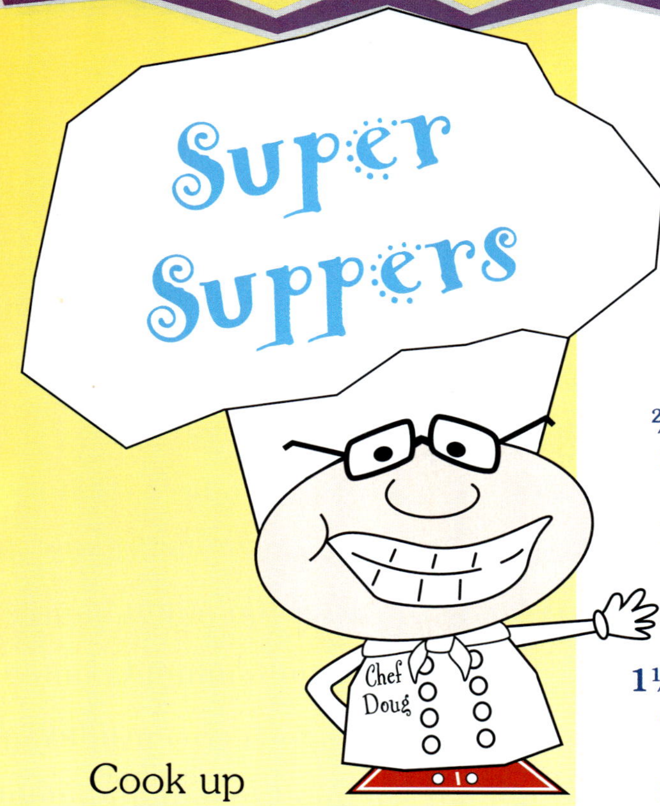

Cook up some fun for dinner tonight! Whether it's pizza or pasta, sandwiches or sides, the whole family will love these recipes (and the kids might even eat their broccoli).

Hot Diggity Dots & Twisters

- **⅔ cup milk**
- **2 tablespoons margarine or butter**
- **1 (4.8-ounce) package PASTA RONI® Four Cheese Flavor with Corkscrew Pasta**
- **1½ cups frozen peas**
- **4 hot dogs, cut into ½-inch pieces**
- **2 teaspoons mustard**

1. In large saucepan, bring 1¼ cups water, milk and margarine just to a boil.
2. Stir in pasta, peas and Special Seasonings; return to a boil. Reduce heat to medium. Gently boil uncovered, 7 to 8 minutes or until pasta is tender, stirring occasionally.
3. Stir in hot dogs and mustard. Let stand 3 to 5 minutes before serving.

Makes 4 servings

Prep Time: 5 minutes
Cook Time: 15 minutes

Hot Diggity Dots & Twisters

Sausage Cheeseburger Pizza

1 pound BOB EVANS® Original Recipe Roll Sausage
1 (12-inch) prepared pizza shell
½ cup yellow mustard
2 cups (8 ounces) shredded mozzarella cheese
½ cup chopped onion
15 dill pickle slices
¾ cup (3 ounces) shredded Cheddar cheese

Preheat oven to 425°F. Crumble and cook sausage in medium skillet until browned; drain well on paper towels. Place pizza shell on lightly greased 12-inch pizza pan or baking sheet. Spread mustard over shell; top with mozzarella cheese, sausage and onion. Place pickle slices evenly on top; sprinkle with Cheddar cheese. Bake 12 minutes or until crust is cooked through and cheese is bubbly. Cut into thin wedges or squares and serve hot. Refrigerate leftovers.

Makes about 8 servings

Green Beans Orange

1 pound fresh *or* 2 (9-ounce) packages frozen whole green beans
¼ cup SMUCKER'S® Low Sugar Orange Marmalade
1 teaspoon lemon juice

Cut ends off green beans; wash. Cover and cook in a small amount of boiling salted water until tender-crisp, about 5 minutes. Drain. (Or cook frozen green beans according to package directions; drain.)

Add marmalade and lemon juice. Cook and gently stir until beans are coated and hot. *Makes 6 servings*

Sausage Cheeseburger Pizza

Cheesy Tuna Mac

8 ounces uncooked elbow macaroni
2 tablespoons margarine or butter
2 tablespoons all-purpose flour
1 teaspoon paprika
¼ teaspoon salt
1 cup canned reduced-sodium chicken broth
6 ounces reduced-fat reduced-sodium cheese spread, cut into cubes
1 can (6 ounces) tuna packed in water, drained and flaked

1. Cook macaroni according to package directions, omitting salt. Drain; set aside.

2. Melt margarine in medium saucepan over medium heat. Add flour, paprika and salt; cook and stir 1 minute. Add broth; bring to a simmer for 2 minutes or until sauce thickens.

3. Add cheese spread; cook and stir until cheese melts. Combine tuna and pasta in medium bowl; pour sauce mixture over tuna mixture; toss to coat. Garnish with additional paprika, if desired.

Makes 4 servings

Cheesy Tuna Mac

Sweet and Sour Chicken Nuggets

- 2 (1-cup) bags UNCLE BEN'S® Brand Boil-in-Bag Rice
- 1 package (10 ounces) frozen chicken nuggets or chicken chunks
- 1 tablespoon oil
- 2 large green bell peppers, cut into 1-inch squares
- 2 large carrots, diagonally cut into thin slices
- 1½ teaspoons minced garlic
- 2 cans (8 ounces each) pineapple chunks in juice, drained and ½ cup juice reserved
- 1 jar (10 ounces) sweet and sour sauce

1. Cook rice according to package directions.

2. Prepare chicken nuggets according to package directions for conventional oven.

3. Heat oil in large skillet over medium-high heat until hot. Add bell peppers, carrots and garlic; cook and stir 4 minutes. Add reserved pineapple juice. Cover; reduce heat and simmer 10 to 12 minutes until vegetables are almost tender. Add pineapple chunks; cover and cook 2 minutes. Stir in sweet and sour sauce; cover and cook 2 more minutes or until hot.

4. Place warm chicken nuggets on a bed of rice and top with vegetable mixture.

Makes 4 servings

Funny Face Pizzas

1 package (10 ounces) refrigerated pizza dough
1 cup pizza sauce
1 cup (4 ounces) shredded mozzarella cheese
Assorted toppings: pepperoni, black olive slices, green or red bell pepper slices, mushroom slices
⅓ cup shredded Cheddar cheese

Heat oven to 425°F. Spray baking sheet with nonstick cooking spray; set aside.

Remove dough from package. *Do not unroll dough.* Slice dough into 4 equal pieces. Knead each piece of dough until ball forms. Pat or roll each ball into 4-inch disk. Place disks on prepared baking sheet.

Spread ¼ cup sauce on each disk. Sprinkle with mozzarella cheese. Decorate with toppings to create faces. Sprinkle with Cheddar cheese to resemble hair.

Bake 10 minutes or until cheese is just melted and bottoms of pizzas are light brown. *Makes 4 servings*

SPAM™ Sticks

1 (12-ounce) can SPAM® Luncheon Meat
1 egg
2 tablespoons milk
2 tablespoons all-purpose flour
½ cup soda cracker crumbs

Heat oven to 375°F. Slice SPAM® into 8 pieces; cut each slice in half lengthwise. Beat together egg and milk. Coat each SPAM® slice with flour. Dip in milk mixture and roll in cracker crumbs. Place on baking sheet. Bake 15 to 18 minutes or until golden brown. Serve with tartar sauce or ketchup. *Makes 4 servings*

Hearty BBQ Beef Sandwiches

1 envelope LIPTON® RECIPE SECRETS® Onion Soup Mix
2 cups water
½ cup chili sauce
¼ cup firmly packed light brown sugar
1 (3-pound) boneless chuck roast
8 kaiser rolls or hamburger buns, toasted

1. Preheat oven to 325°F. In Dutch oven or 5-quart heavy ovenproof saucepot, combine soup mix, water, chili sauce and sugar; add roast.

2. Cover and bake 3 hours or until roast is tender.

3. Remove roast; reserve juices. Bring reserved juices to a boil over high heat. Boil 4 minutes.

4. Meanwhile, with fork, shred roast. Stir roast into reserved juices and simmer, stirring frequently, 1 minute. Serve on rolls.

Makes 8 servings

Recipe Tip: Always measure brown sugar in a dry measure cup and pack down firmly. To soften hardened brown sugar, place in glass dish with 1 slice of bread. Cover with plastic wrap and microwave at HIGH 30 to 40 seconds. Let stand 30 seconds; stir. Remove bread.

Hearty BBQ Beef Sandwich

Amigo Pita Pocket Sandwiches

1 pound ground turkey
1 can (7 ounces) whole kernel corn, drained
1 can (6 ounces) tomato paste
½ cup water
½ cup chopped green bell pepper
1 package (1.0 ounce) LAWRY'S® Taco Spices & Seasonings
8 pita breads
Curly lettuce leaves
Shredded cheddar cheese

In large skillet, brown ground turkey until no longer pink; drain fat. Add corn, tomato paste, water, green pepper and Taco Spices & Seasonings; mix well. Bring to a boil over medium-high heat; reduce heat to low and cook, uncovered, 15 minutes. Cut off top quarter of pita breads and open to form pockets. Line each with lettuce leaves. Spoon about ½ cup filling into each pita bread and top with cheese.
Makes 8 servings

Serving Suggestion: Serve with vegetable sticks and fresh fruit.

Campbell's® Cheesy Broccoli

1 can (10¾ ounces) CAMPBELL'S® Condensed Cheddar Cheese Soup
¼ cup milk
4 cups frozen broccoli cuts

1. In 2-quart microwave-safe casserole mix soup and milk. Add broccoli.

2. Cover and microwave on HIGH 8 minutes or until broccoli is tender-crisp, stirring once during heating. *Makes 4 servings*

Prep/Cook Time: 10 minutes

Amigo Pita Pocket Sandwiches

Cowboy Burgers

1 pound ground beef
½ teaspoon LAWRY'S® Seasoned Salt
½ teaspoon LAWRY'S® Seasoned Pepper
2 tablespoons plus 2 teaspoons butter OR margarine
1 large onion, thinly sliced
1 package (1.0 ounces) LAWRY'S® Taco Spices & Seasonings
4 slices cheddar cheese
4 Kaiser rolls
Lettuce leaves
Tomato slices

In medium bowl, combine ground beef, Seasoned Salt and Seasoned Pepper; shape into four patties. Grill or broil to desired doneness (about 5 to 6 minutes on each side for medium). Meanwhile, in medium skillet, melt butter. Add onion and Taco Spices & Seasonings; mix well. Cook onion over medium-high heat until soft and transparent. Top each patty with onions and cheese. Return to grill or broiler until cheese is melted. Place each patty on roll; top with lettuce and tomato. *Makes 4 servings*

Serving Suggestion: Serve with baked beans.

Cowboy Burger

Tic-Tac-Toe Tuna Pizza

1 bread-style prepared pizza crust (10 ounces)
1 can (12 ounces) tuna packed in water, drained
½ cup minced onion
⅓ cup reduced-fat mayonnaise
9 thin plum tomato slices
4 to 5 slices (¾ ounce each) process cheese food or American cheese

1. Preheat oven to 425°F. Place pizza crust on pizza pan or baking sheet.

2. Combine tuna, onion and mayonnaise in medium bowl; season to taste with salt and pepper. Stir until blended. Spread mixture over crust, leaving 1-inch border. Arrange tomato slices on tuna mixture in 3 rows, spacing at least ½ inch apart.

3. Bake 10 to 12 minutes or until heated through.

4. While pizza is baking, cut cheese slices into ½-inch-wide strips.

5. Remove pizza from oven. Arrange enough strips over tuna mixture to resemble tic-tac-toe game. Crisscross remaining strips over some tomato slices. Let stand 5 minutes before serving.

Makes 6 servings

Prep and Cook Time: 30 minutes

Tic-Tac-Toe Tuna Pizza

Sugar and spice and everything nice! That's what these yummy goodies are made of. Scrumptious cookies, cupcakes and desserts will tempt anyone who has eaten all their vegetables.

Dish of Dirt

- 14 OREO® Chocolate Sandwich Cookies, finely crushed (about 1 cup crumbs), divided
- 1 pint chocolate ice cream
- ¼ cup chocolate-flavored syrup
- Gummy worms, for garnish
- Prepared whipped topping, for garnish

In each of 4 dessert dishes, place 2 tablespoons cookie crumbs. Top each with ½ cup ice cream, remaining 2 tablespoons cookie crumbs and 1 tablespoon syrup. Garnish with gummy worms and whipped topping.

Makes 4 servings

Dish of Dirt

Peanut Butter and Jelly Sandwich Cookies

1 package (about 18 ounces) refrigerated sugar cookie dough
1 tablespoon unsweetened cocoa powder
All-purpose flour (optional)
1¾ cups creamy peanut butter
½ cup grape jam or jelly

1. Remove dough from wrapper according to package directions. Reserve ¼ of dough; cover and refrigerate remaining ¾ of dough. Combine reserved dough and cocoa in small bowl; refrigerate.

2. Shape remaining ¾ dough into 5½-inch log. Sprinkle with flour to minimize sticking, if necessary. Remove chocolate dough from refrigerator; roll on sheet of waxed paper to 9½×6½-inch rectangle. Place dough log in center of rectangle.

3. Bring waxed paper edges and chocolate dough up and together over log. Press gently on top and sides of dough so entire log is wrapped in chocolate dough. Flatten log slightly to form square. Wrap in waxed paper. Freeze 10 minutes.

4. Preheat oven to 350°F. Remove waxed paper from dough. Cut dough into ¼-inch slices. Place slices 2 inches apart on ungreased cookie sheets. Reshape dough edges into square, if necessary. Press dough slightly to form indentation so dough resembles slice of bread.

5. Bake 8 to 11 minutes or until lightly browned. Remove from oven and straighten cookie edges with spatula. Cool 2 minutes on cookie sheets. Remove to wire racks; cool completely.

6. To make sandwich, spread about 1 tablespoon peanut butter on underside of 1 cookie. Spread about ½ tablespoon jam over peanut butter; top with second cookie, pressing gently. Repeat with remaining cookies. *Makes 11 sandwich cookies*

Peanut Butter and Jelly Sandwich Cookies

Baker's® One Bowl® G'me S'more Brownies!

9 whole graham crackers
4 squares BAKER'S® Unsweetened Baking Chocolate
¾ cup (1½ sticks) butter *or* margarine
2 cups sugar
3 eggs
1 teaspoon vanilla
1 cup flour
1 package (10½ ounces) miniature marshmallows
1 package (11 ounces) BAKER'S® Milk Chocolate Chips

HEAT oven to 350°F. Line bottom of greased 13×9-inch baking pan with graham crackers.

MICROWAVE chocolate and butter in large microwavable bowl on HIGH 2 minutes or until butter is melted. Stir until chocolate is completely melted.

STIR sugar into chocolate mixture until well blended. Mix in eggs and vanilla. Stir in flour until well blended. Spread over crackers in prepared pan.

BAKE 30 to 35 minutes or until toothpick inserted in center comes out with fudgy crumbs. *Do not overbake.* Sprinkle marshmallows and chocolate chips evenly over top of brownies. Return to oven 5 minutes or just until marshmallows begin to melt together. Cool completely. *Makes 24 brownies*

Tip: For ease in cutting, dip knife in warm water and wipe dry between cuts.

Prep Time: 10 minutes
Bake Time: 40 minutes

Hollywood Walk of Fame Stars

1 (12-ounce) package milk chocolate chips
1 (12-ounce) package butterscotch chips
½ cup PETER PAN® Crunchy Peanut Butter
1 bag popped ORVILLE REDENBACHER'S® REDENBUDDERS® MOVIE THEATER BUTTER POPPING CORN, unpopped kernels discarded
1 cup cornflakes cereal
1 cup honey graham cereal
WESSON® No-Stick Cooking Spray
Large star-shaped cookie cutter

1. Melt chocolate and butterscotch chips in large saucepan over low heat.

2. Stir in peanut butter until smooth. Remove from heat. Stir in popcorn, cornflakes and graham cereal. Coat evenly.

3. Line 15½×10-inch jelly roll pan with foil. Lightly spray with cooking spray.

4. Spread popcorn mixture evenly in pan. Refrigerate 15 minutes.

5. Spray cookie cutter with cooking spray.

6. Carefully press out stars. Store in refrigerator.

Makes 12 medium or 6 to 8 large stars

Total Preparation Time: 50 minutes

Ice Cream Cone Cakes

1 package (18¼ ounces) devil's food cake mix plus ingredients to prepare mix
⅓ cup sour cream
1 package flat-bottomed ice cream cones (about 18 cones)
1¼ cups nonfat frozen yogurt (any flavor)
Cake decorations or chocolate sprinkles

1. Preheat oven to 350°F. Grease and flour 8- or 9-inch round cake pan; set aside.

2. Prepare cake mix according to package directions, substituting sour cream for ⅓ cup of the water and decreasing oil to ¼ cup.

3. Spoon ½ of the batter (about 2⅓ cups) evenly into ice cream cones, using about 2 tablespoons batter for each. Pour remaining batter into prepared cake pan.

4. Stand cones on cookie sheet. Bake cones and cake layer until toothpick inserted into center of cake comes out clean, about 20 minutes for cones and about 35 minutes for cake layer. Cool on wire racks, removing cake from pan after 10 minutes. Reserve or freeze cake layer for another use.

5. Top each filled cone with ¼ cup scoop of frozen yogurt just before serving. Sprinkle with decorations as desired. Serve immediately.

Makes 18 servings

Ice Cream Cone Cakes

Wild Side Sundaes

4 packages (4-serving size) JELL-O® Brand Gelatin, 4 different flavors
4 cups boiling water
2 cups cold water
1 tub (8 ounces) COOL WHIP® Whipped Topping, thawed
Additional thawed COOL WHIP® Whipped Topping

DISSOLVE each package of gelatin completely in 1 cup boiling water in separate bowls. Stir ½ cup cold water into each bowl of gelatin. Pour each mixture into separate 8-inch square pans. Refrigerate at least 3 hours or until firm. Cut gelatin in each pan into ½-inch cubes.

LAYER gelatin cubes alternately with whipped topping in sundae glasses. Garnish with dollop of additional whipped topping.

REFRIGERATE until ready to serve. *Makes 16 servings*

Wild Side Sundaes

Cookies & Cream Cupcakes

2¼ cups all-purpose flour
1 tablespoon baking powder
½ teaspoon salt
1⅔ cups sugar
1 cup milk
½ cup butter, softened
2 teaspoons vanilla
3 egg whites
1 cup crushed chocolate sandwich cookies (about 10 cookies) plus additional for garnish
1 (16-ounce) container prepared vanilla frosting

1. Preheat oven to 350°F. Line 24 regular-size (2½-inch) muffin pan cups with paper muffin cup liners.

2. Sift flour, baking powder and salt together in large bowl. Stir in sugar. Add milk, butter and vanilla; beat with electric mixer at low speed 30 seconds. Beat at medium speed 2 minutes. Add egg whites; beat 2 minutes. Stir in 1 cup crushed cookies.

3. Spoon batter into prepared muffin pans. Bake 20 to 25 minutes or until toothpick inserted into centers comes out clean. Cool in pans on wire racks 10 minutes. Remove to racks; cool completely.

4. Frost cupcakes; garnish with additional crushed cookies.

Makes 24 cupcakes

Cookies & Cream Cupcakes

Letters of the Alphabet

Gingerbread Cookie Dough (recipe follows)
Colored frostings and glazes, colored sugars, sprinkles and assorted small candies

1. Prepare Gingerbread Cookie Dough. Cover; refrigerate about 8 hours or until firm.

2. Preheat oven to 350°F. Grease cookie sheets.

3. Divide dough into 4 equal sections. Reserve 1 section; refrigerate remaining 3 sections.

4. Roll reserved dough on well-floured surface to ⅛-inch thickness. Sprinkle with flour to minimize sticking, if necessary.

5. Cut out alphabet letter shapes using 2½-inch cookie cutters. Place cut out cookies on cookie sheet. Repeat steps with remaining dough.

6. Bake 6 to 8 minutes or until edges begin to brown. Remove cookies to wire racks; cool completely.

7. Decorate cookies with frostings, glazes, colored sugars, sprinkles and assorted small candies. *Makes about 5 dozen cookies*

Gingerbread Cookie Dough

½ cup shortening
⅓ cup packed light brown sugar
¼ cup dark molasses
1 egg white
½ teaspoon vanilla
1½ cups all-purpose flour
1 teaspoon ground cinnamon
½ teaspoon baking soda
½ teaspoon salt
½ teaspoon ground ginger
¼ teaspoon baking powder

1. Beat shortening, brown sugar, molasses, egg white and vanilla in large bowl at high speed of electric mixer until smooth.

2. Combine flour, cinnamon, baking soda, salt, ginger and baking powder in small bowl. Add to shortening mixture; mix well. Cover; refrigerate about 8 hours or until firm.

Brownie Sandwich Cookies

BROWNIE COOKIES

1 package DUNCAN HINES® Chocolate Lovers Double Fudge Brownie Mix
1 egg
3 tablespoons water
Sugar

FILLING

1 container (16 ounces) DUNCAN HINES® Creamy Homestyle Cream Cheese Frosting
Red food coloring (optional)
½ cup semisweet mini chocolate chips

1. Preheat oven to 375°F. Grease cookie sheets.

2. For brownie cookies, combine brownie mix, fudge packet from mix, egg and water in large bowl. Stir until well blended, about 50 strokes. Shape dough into 50 (1-inch) balls. Place 2 inches apart on prepared cookie sheets. Grease bottom of drinking glass; dip in sugar. Press gently to flatten 1 cookie to ⅜-inch thickness. Repeat with remaining cookies. Bake at 375°F for 6 to 7 minutes or until set. Cool 1 minute on cookie sheets. Remove to cooling racks. Cool completely.

3. For filling, tint frosting with red food coloring, if desired. Stir in chocolate chips.

4. To assemble, spread 1 tablespoon frosting on bottom of one cookie; top with second cookie. Press together to make sandwich cookie. Repeat with remaining cookies.

Makes 25 sandwich cookies

Brownie Sandwich Cookies

Mud Slides

2 cups cold milk
1 package (4-serving size) JELL-O® Chocolate Flavor Instant Pudding & Pie Filling
14 chocolate sandwich cookies, finely crushed (about 1½ cups)
2 cups thawed COOL WHIP® Whipped Topping

LINE bottoms and sides of 2 loaf pans with wet paper towels. Tilt 2 (12-ounce) glasses in each pan.

POUR milk into 1-quart container with tight-fitting lid. Add pudding mix; cover tightly. Shake vigorously at least 45 seconds; pour evenly into glasses.

GENTLY stir 1¼ cups of the cookies into whipped topping with wire whisk in medium bowl until blended. Spoon evenly over pudding in glasses; sprinkle with remaining ¼ cup cookies.

REFRIGERATE until ready to serve. *Makes 4 servings*

Mud Slide

Perfect Parties

Looking for some new ideas for your child's next party? Choose from four fun menus with tasty recipes to make your tyke's next birthday or celebration easy for you and memorable for them.

- **Backyard Camp-out**
- **Slumber Party**
- **Fairy Princess Party**
- **Under the Sea Party**

Campfire Hot Dogs

$\frac{1}{2}$ pound ground beef
2 cups RAGÚ® Old World Style® Pasta Sauce
1 can ($10\frac{3}{4}$ to 16 ounces) baked beans
8 frankfurters, cooked
8 frankfurter rolls

1. In 12-inch skillet, brown ground beef over medium-high heat; drain.

2. Stir in Ragú Pasta Sauce and beans. Bring to a boil over high heat. Reduce heat to low and simmer, stirring occasionally, 5 minutes.

3. To serve, arrange frankfurters in rolls and top with sauce mixture. Garnish, if desired, with Cheddar cheese.

Makes 8 servings

Tip: For Chili Campfire Hot Dogs, simply stir 2 to 3 teaspoon chili powder into sauce mixture.

Prep Time: 5 minutes
Cook Time: 10 minutes

BACKYARD CAMP-OUT

- Campfire Hot Dogs
- Campbell's® Cheddary Pouch Potatoes
- S'mores

Campfire Hot Dogs

Campbell's® Cheddary Pouch Potatoes

- 1 can (10¾ ounces) CAMPBELL'S® Condensed Cheddar Cheese Soup
- ¼ cup milk
- ½ teaspoon garlic powder
- ¼ teaspoon onion powder
- 4 cups frozen steak fries
- Paprika

1. In large bowl mix soup, milk, garlic powder and onion powder. Stir in potatoes.

2. Cut four 14-inch squares of heavy-duty aluminum foil. Spoon ***1 cup*** soup mixture onto each square, arranging potatoes to make a single layer. Sprinkle with paprika. Bring up sides of foil and double fold. Double fold ends to make packet.

3. Place potato packets on grill rack over medium-hot coals. Grill 25 minutes or until potatoes are tender. *Makes 4 servings*

Campbell's® Cheddary Oven Pouch Potatoes: In Step 3, on baking sheet bake packets at 350°F. for 25 minutes.

Prep Time: 5 minutes
Cook Time: 25 minutes

S'Mores

16 graham cracker squares
4 milk chocolate bars (1.55 ounces each), halved
1 cup miniature marshmallows

1. Preheat broiler.

2. Arrange half of graham crackers on baking sheet. Top each cracker with 1 piece of the chocolate bars. Broil until chocolate is softened but not melted.

3. Arrange 2 tablespoons marshmallows on each cracker. Broil until lightly toasted.

4. Top with remaining crackers and serve. *Makes 8 s'mores*

Campbell's® Cheddary Pouch Potatoes

Smushy Cookies

1 package (20 ounces) refrigerated cookie dough, any flavor
All-purpose flour (optional)
Peanut butter, multi-colored miniature marshmallows, assorted colored sprinkles, chocolate-covered raisins and caramel candy squares

1. Preheat oven to 350°F. Grease cookie sheets.

2. Remove dough from wrapper according to package directions. Cut into 4 equal sections. Reserve 1 section; refrigerate remaining 3 sections.

3. Roll reserved dough to ¼-inch thickness. Sprinkle with flour to minimize sticking, if necessary. Cut out cookies using 2½-inch round cookie cutter. Transfer to prepared cookie sheets. Repeat with remaining dough, working with 1 section at a time.

4. Bake 8 to 11 minutes or until edges are light golden brown. Remove to wire racks; cool completely.

5. To make sandwich, spread about 1½ tablespoons peanut butter on underside of 1 cookie to within ¼ inch of edge. Sprinkle with miniature marshmallows and candy pieces. Top with second cookie, pressing gently. Repeat with remaining cookies and fillings.

6. Just before serving, place sandwiches on paper towels. Microwave at HIGH 15 to 25 seconds or until fillings become soft.

Makes about 8 to 10 sandwich cookies

Slumber Party

- Chili Chip Party Platter
- Cinnamon RedHot® Popcorn
- Smushy Cookies

Smushy Cookies

Chili Chip Party Platter

1 pound ground beef
1 medium onion, chopped
1 package (1.48 ounces) LAWRY'S® Spices & Seasonings for Chili
1 can (6 ounces) tomato paste
1 cup water
1 bag (8 to 9 ounces) tortilla chips or corn chips
1½ cups (6 ounces) shredded cheddar cheese
1 can (2¼ ounces) sliced pitted black olives, drained
½ cup sliced green onions

In medium skillet, cook ground beef until browned and crumbly; drain fat. Add onion, Spices & Seasonings for Chili, tomato paste and water; mix well. Bring to a boil over medium-high heat. Reduce heat to low; simmer, uncovered, 15 minutes, stirring occasionally. Serve over tortilla chips. Top with cheddar cheese, olives and green onion.

Makes 4 servings

Serving Suggestion: Serve with a cool beverage and sliced melon.

Chili Chip Party Platter

Cinnamon RedHot® Popcorn

10 cups air-popped popcorn (½ cup unpopped)
1½ cups (7 ounces) coarsely chopped pecans
¾ cup granulated sugar
¾ cup packed light brown sugar
½ cup light corn syrup
3 tablespoons *Frank's® RedHot®* Sauce
2 tablespoons honey
6 tablespoons (¾ stick) unsalted butter, at room temperature, cut into thin pats
1 tablespoon ground cinnamon

1. Preheat oven to 250°F. Place popcorn and pecans in 5-quart ovenproof bowl or Dutch oven. Bake 15 minutes.

2. Combine sugars, corn syrup, ***RedHot*** Sauce and honey in 2-quart saucepan. Bring to a full boil over medium-high heat, stirring just until sugars dissolve. Boil about 6 to 8 minutes or until soft crack stage (290°F on candy thermometer). *Do not stir.* Remove from heat.

3. Gradually add butter and cinnamon to sugar mixture, stirring gently until well blended. Pour over popcorn, tossing to coat evenly.* Spread popcorn mixture on greased baking sheets, using two forks. Cool completely. Break into bite-size pieces. Store in airtight container up to 2 weeks. *Makes 18 cups*

**If popcorn mixture sets too quickly, return to oven to rewarm. Popcorn mixture may be shaped into 3-inch balls while warm, if desired.*

Prep Time: 15 minutes
Cook Time: 8 to 10 minutes

Cinnamon RedHot® Popcorn

Dream Castle

5¼ cups Buttercream Frosting (page 234)
Blue and yellow food color
3 (8-inch) square cakes, tops and edges trimmed
2 cups Base Frosting (page 234), optional
Assorted colored sugar
4 sugar ice cream cones
Small purple and white gumdrops
Pastel candy-coated chocolate pieces
2 pink sugar wafer cookies
1 (19×13-inch) cake board, cut in half crosswise and covered

1. Color ½ cup Buttercream Frosting blue and ½ cup yellow; reserve 4¼ cups white frosting. Place one square cake on prepared cake board. Frost top with some of the white frosting.

2. Cut remaining cakes as shown in diagrams 1 and 2 (see page 234).

3. Place piece A over bottom layer. Frost top of piece A with some of the white frosting. Position remaining pieces as shown in diagram 3 (see page 234), connecting with some of the white frosting.

4. Frost entire cake with Base Frosting to seal in crumbs. Frost again with white frosting. Cover piece D (bridge) with colored sugar.

5. Frost cones with blue and yellow frostings. Place as shown.

6. Decorate as shown, using frosting to attach candies, if needed. Arrange wafer cookies on front of castle for gate.

Makes 24 to 28 servings

Continued on page 234

Fairy Princess Party

- small sandwiches cut into flower and butterfly shapes
- Magic Wands
- Dream Castle

Dream Castle

Dream Castle, continued

Buttercream Frosting

6 cups powdered sugar, sifted and divided
¾ cup butter or margarine, softened
¼ cup shortening
6 to 8 tablespoons milk, divided
1 teaspoon vanilla extract

Place 3 cups sugar, butter, shortening, 4 tablespoons milk and vanilla in large bowl. Beat with electric mixer until smooth. Add remaining 3 cups powdered sugar; beat at medium speed until light and fluffy, adding more milk, 1 tablespoon at a time, as needed for good spreading consistency. *Makes about 3½ cups frosting*

Base Frosting

3 cups powdered sugar, sifted
½ cup shortening
¼ cup milk plus additional, if necessary
½ teaspoon vanilla

Combine sugar, shortening, ¼ cup milk and vanilla in large bowl. Beat with electric mixer on medium speed until smooth. Add more milk, 1 teaspoon at a time, until frosting is a thin consistency. Use frosting immediately. *Makes about 2 cups*

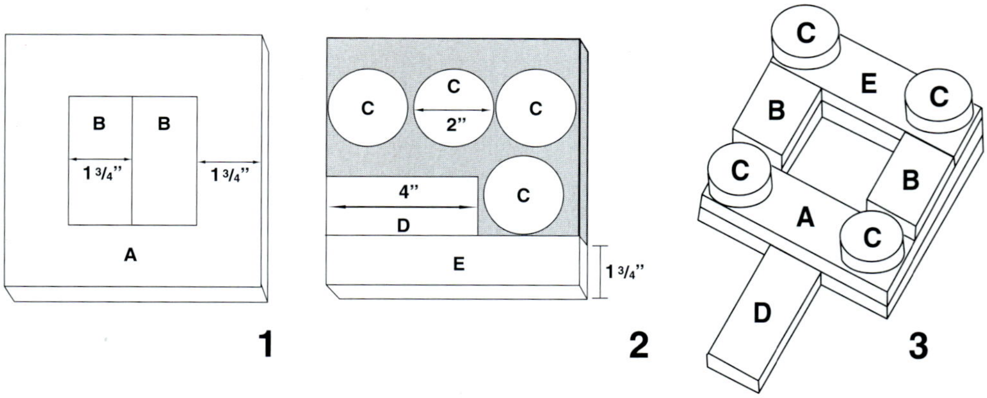

Magic Wands

1 cup semisweet chocolate chips
12 pretzel rods
3 ounces white chocolate baking bars or almond bark
Red and yellow food color
Assorted sprinkles

1. Line baking sheet with waxed paper.

2. Melt semisweet chocolate in top of double boiler over hot, not boiling, water. Remove from heat. Dip pretzel rods into chocolate, spooning chocolate to coat about ¾ of each pretzel. Place on prepared baking sheet. Refrigerate until chocolate is firm.

3. Melt white chocolate in top of clean double boiler over hot, not boiling, water. Stir in food colors to make orange. Remove from heat. Dip coated pretzels quickly into colored chocolate to coat about ¼ of each pretzel.

4. Place on baking sheet. Immediately top with sprinkles. Refrigerate until chocolate is firm.

5. Tie ends with ribbons.

Makes 12 wands

Octo-Dogs and Shells

4 hot dogs
1½ cups uncooked small shell pasta
1½ cups frozen mixed vegetables
1 cup prepared Alfredo sauce
Prepared yellow mustard in squeeze bottle
Cheese-flavored fish-shaped crackers

Lay 1 hot dog on side with end facing you. Starting 1 inch from one end of hot dog, slice hot dog vertically in half. Roll hot dog ¼ turn and slice in half vertically again, making 4 segments connected at the top. Slice each segment in half vertically, creating a total of 8 "legs." Repeat with remaining hot dogs.

Place hot dogs in medium saucepan; cover with water. Bring to a boil over medium-high heat. Remove from heat; set aside.

Prepare pasta according to package directions, stirring in vegetables during last 3 minutes of cooking time. Drain; return to pan. Stir in Alfredo sauce. Heat over low heat until heated through. Divide pasta mixture between four plates.

Drain "octo-dogs." Arrange one octo-dog on top of pasta mixture on each plate. Draw faces on "heads" of octo-dogs with mustard. Sprinkle crackers over pasta mixture. *Makes 4 servings*

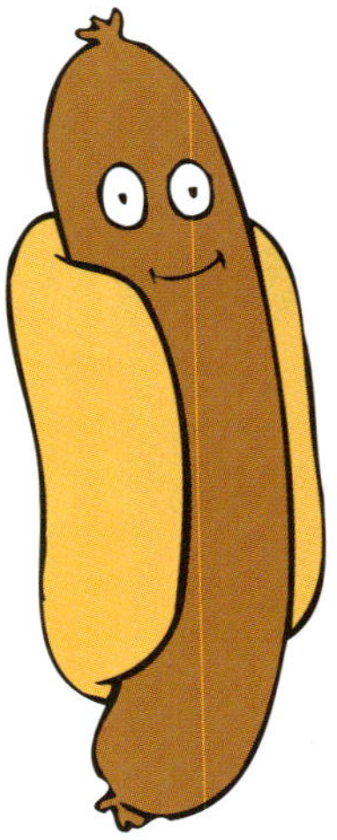

Under the Sea

- Octo-Dogs and Shells
- blue gelatin blocks with gummy fish
- School-of-Fish Cake

Octo-Dog and Shells

School-of-Fish Cake

1 (13×9-inch) cake
1 recipe Creamy White Frosting (page 240)
Blue paste food coloring
1 recipe Base Frosting (page 234)
Large and small gumdrops
1 (19×13-inch) cake board, cut to fit cake if desired, covered

1. If cake top is rounded, trim horizontally with long serrated knife. Trim sides of cake. Place cake on prepared cake board.

2. Tint Creamy White Frosting blue by adding small amount of desired paste color with toothpick; stir well. Slowly add more color until frosting is desired shade.

3. Frost top and sides of cake with Base Frosting to seal in crumbs. Frost again with blue frosting. Swirl frosting to resemble waves.

4. To make large fish, position 1 large gumdrop on cutting board and cut lengthwise in half. Set aside 1 gumdrop half for fish body. For tail, place remaining gumdrop half, cut side down, on cutting board. Cut wedge piece from center of wide end (see photo 1, page 240). Place fish body in desired position on cake top. Place narrow end of tail piece next to wide end of fish body (see photo 2, page 240). Trim reserved wedge piece into fin shape and place above body of fish.

5. For eyes and bubbles, cut off small pieces of gumdrop and press onto fish and cake. Decorate fish by cutting additional small pieces of gumdrop and pressing pieces onto fish, if desired. Repeat with additional large gumdrops to make more large fish. Repeat with small gumdrops to make small fish. *Makes 16 to 20 servings*

Continued on page 240

School-of-Fish Cake

School-of-Fish Cake, continued

1. Trim piece into fin shape.

2. Place tail next to fish body.

Creamy White Frosting

- ½ cup shortening
- 6 cups sifted powdered sugar, divided
- 3 tablespoons milk
- 2 teaspoons clear vanilla extract
- Additional milk*

**For thinner frosting, use more milk and for thicker frosting use less milk.*

Beat shortening in large bowl with electric mixer at medium speed until fluffy. Gradually beat in 3 cups sugar until well blended and smooth. Carefully beat in 3 tablespoons milk and vanilla. Gradually beat in remaining 3 cups sugar, adding more milk, 1 teaspoon at a time, as needed for good spreading consistency. Store in refrigerator.

Makes enough to fill and frost 2 (8-inch) round or square cake layers or frost 1 (13×9-inch) cake

My Favorites

My Favorite Recipes

Favorite recipe: ______________________

Favorite recipe from: ______________________

Ingredients: ______________________

Method: ______________________

My Favorite Recipes

Favorite recipe: ______________________________

Favorite recipe from: ______________________________

Ingredients: ______________________________

Method: ______________________________

My Favorite Recipes

Favorite recipe: ______________________________

Favorite recipe from: ______________________________

Ingredients: ______________________________

____

____

____

____

____

Method: ______________________________

____

____

____

____

____

____

____

____

____

____

____

____

My Favorite Recipes

Favorite recipe: ______________________

Favorite recipe from: ______________________

Ingredients: ______________________

____

____

____

____

____

Method: ______________________

____

____

____

____

____

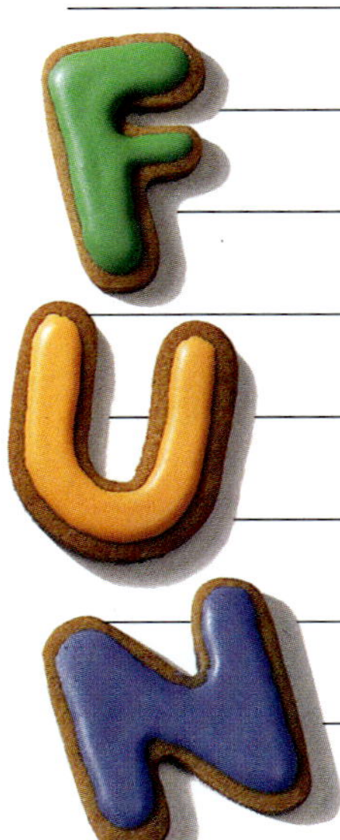

____

____

____

____

____

____

____

My Favorite Recipes

Favorite recipe: ______________________________

Favorite recipe from: ______________________________

Ingredients: ______________________________

____

____

____

____

____

Method: ______________________________

____

____

____

____

____

____

____

____

____

____

____

____

My Favorite Recipes

Favorite recipe: ______________________________

Favorite recipe from: ______________________________

Ingredients: ______________________________

____

____

____

____

____

Method: ______________________________

____

____

____

____

____

____

____

____

____

____

____

My Favorite Recipes

Favorite recipe: ______________________________

Favorite recipe from: ______________________________

Ingredients: ______________________________

Method: ______________________________

My Favorite Recipes

Favorite recipe:

Favorite recipe from:

Ingredients:

Method:

My Favorite Recipes

Favorite recipe: ____________________

Favorite recipe from: ____________________

Ingredients: ____________________

Method: ____________________

My Favorite Recipes

Favorite recipe: ____________________

Favorite recipe from: ____________________

Ingredients: ____________________

Method: ____________________

My Favorite Recipes

Favorite recipe: ______________________________

Favorite recipe from: ______________________________

Ingredients: ______________________________

Method: ______________________________

My Favorite Recipes

Favorite recipe: ____________________

Favorite recipe from: ____________________

Ingredients: ____________________

Method: ____________________

My Favorite Recipes

Favorite recipe: ______________________________

Favorite recipe from: ______________________________

Ingredients: ______________________________

Method: ______________________________

My Favorite Recipes

Favorite recipe: ______________________

Favorite recipe from: ______________________

Ingredients: ______________________

Method: ______________________

My Favorite Recipes

Favorite recipe: ______________________________

Favorite recipe from: ______________________________

Ingredients: ______________________________

Method: ______________________________

My Favorite Recipes

Favorite recipe: ______________________________

Favorite recipe from: ______________________________

Ingredients: ______________________________

Method: ______________________________

My Favorite Recipes

Favorite recipe: ______________________________

Favorite recipe from: ______________________________

Ingredients: ______________________________

____

____

____

____

____

Method: ______________________________

____

____

____

____

____

____

____

____

____

____

____

____

My Favorite Recipes

Favorite recipe: ______________________

Favorite recipe from: ______________________

Ingredients: ______________________

Method: ______________________

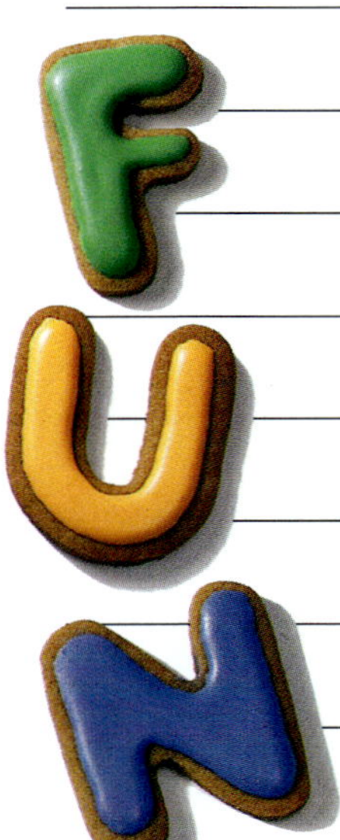

My Favorite Recipes

Favorite recipe: ______________________

Favorite recipe from: ______________________

Ingredients: ______________________

Method: ______________________

My Favorite Recipes

Favorite recipe: ____________________

Favorite recipe from: ____________________

Ingredients: ____________________

____

____

____

____

____

Method: ____________________

____

____

____

____

____

____

____

____

____

____

____

____

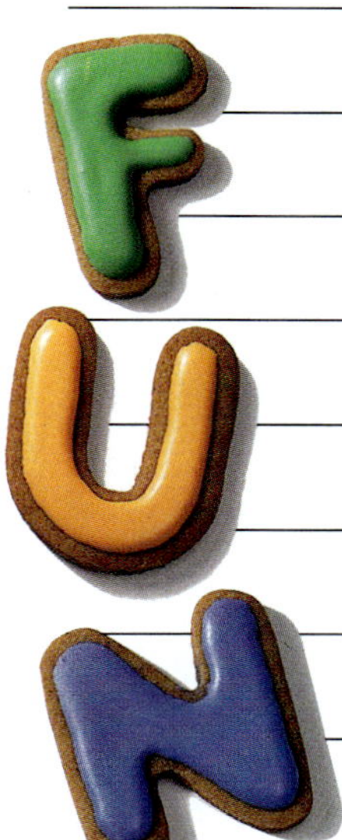

My Favorite Party

Date: ______________________________

What kind of party? ______________________________

____

Who came? ______________________________

____

____

____

____

What did we eat? ______________________________

____

____

____

____

____

____

____

____

____

____

____

____

My Favorite Party

Date: ____

What kind of party? ____________________________

Who came? __________________________________

What did we eat? _____________________________

My Favorite Party

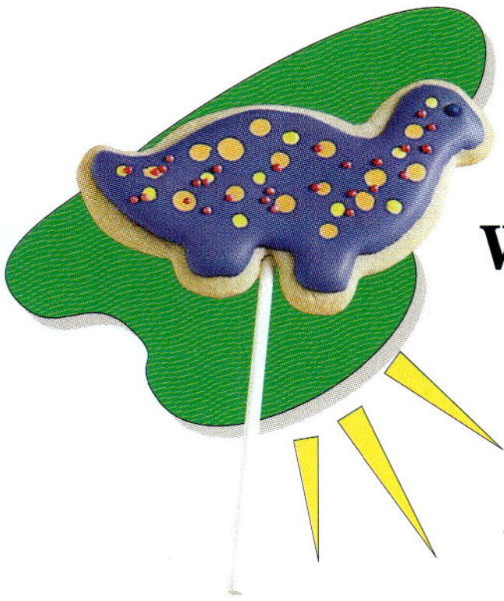

Date: ________________

What kind of party? ________________

____

Who came? ________________

____

____

____

____

What did we eat? ________________

____

____

____

____

____

____

____

____

____

____

____

____

My Favorite Party

Date: ______________________________

What kind of party? ______________________________

____

Who came? ______________________________

____

____

____

____

What did we eat? ______________________________

____

____

____

____

____

____

____

____

____

____

____

____

My Favorite Take-Along Treats

Date: ____________________

Where? ____________________

Who was there? ____________________

____

____

What did I bring? ____________________

____

____

____

____

____

Date: ____________________

Where? ____________________

Who was there? ____________________

____

____

What did I bring? ____________________

____

____

____

____

____

My Favorite Take-Along Treats

Date: ______________________

Where? ______________________

Who was there? ______________________

____

____

What did I bring? ______________________

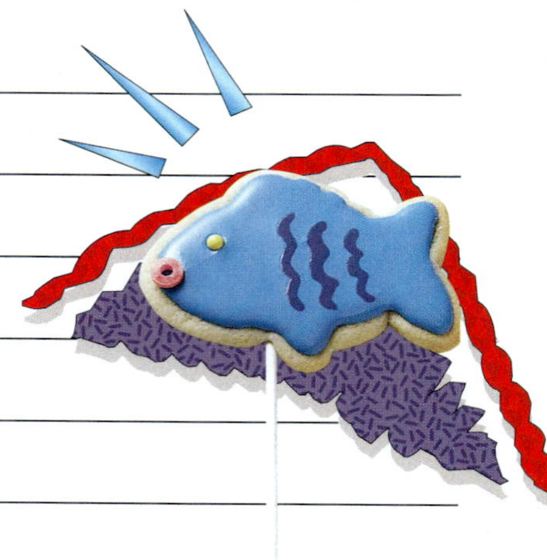

____

____

____

____

____

Date: ______________________

Where? ______________________

Who was there? ______________________

____

____

What did I bring? ______________________

____

____

____

____

____

My Favorite Take-Along Treats

Date: ______________________

Where? ______________________

Who was there? ______________________

____

____

What did I bring? ______________________

____

____

____

____

____

Date: ______________________

Where? ______________________

Who was there? ______________________

____

____

What did I bring? ______________________

____

____

____

____

____

My Favorite Take-Along Treats

Date: ____________________

Where? ____________________

Who was there? ____________________

____

____

What did I bring? ____________________

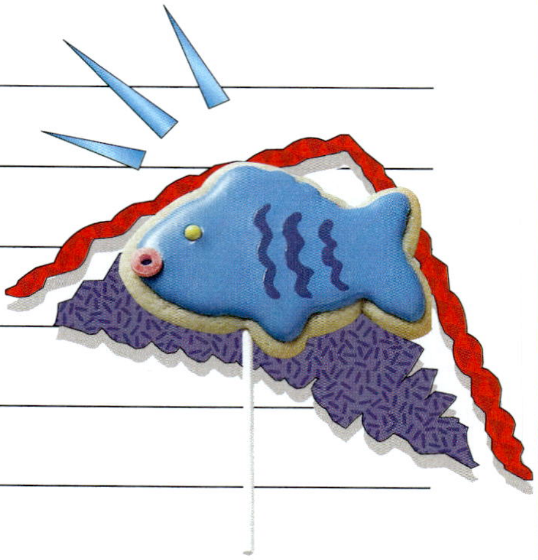

____

____

____

____

____

Date: ____________________

Where? ____________________

Who was there? ____________________

____

____

What did I bring? ____________________

____

____

____

____

____

My Favorite Friends

Friend: ____________________

They love: ____________________

____

____

They don't like: ____________________

____

____

Friend: ____________________

They love: ____________________

____

____

They don't like: ____________________

____

____

Friend: ____________________

They love: ____________________

____

____

They don't like: ____________________

____

____

My Favorite Friends

Friend: ____________________

They love: ____________________

____

____

They don't like: ____________________

____

____

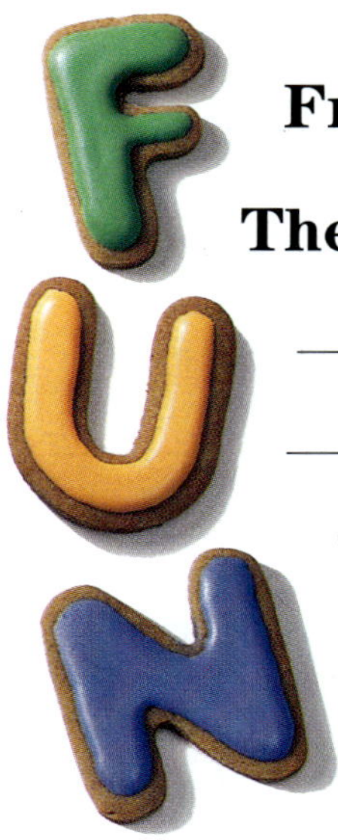

Friend: ____________________

They love: ____________________

____

____

They don't like: ____________________

____

____

Friend: ____________________

They love: ____________________

____

____

They don't like: ____________________

____

____

My Favorite Friends

Friend: ______________________________

They love: ______________________________

____

____

They don't like: ______________________________

____

____

Friend: ______________________________

They love: ______________________________

____

____

They don't like: ______________________________

____

____

Friend: ______________________________

They love: ______________________________

____

____

They don't like: ______________________________

____

____

My Favorite Friends

Friend: ______________________

They love: ______________________

____

____

They don't like: ______________________

____

____

Friend: ______________________

They love: ______________________

____

____

They don't like: ______________________

____

____

Friend: ______________________

They love: ______________________

____

____

They don't like: ______________________

____

____

Hints, Tips & Index

Cake Basics

SPECIAL CAKE EQUIPMENT
Some cakes use decorating techniques that may require special cake decorating equipment. The right equipment not only makes decorating easier, but also gives more professional results.

Flexible metal spatulas of various sizes are useful in applying frosting and creating very smooth surfaces.

Wooden toothpicks are useful for marking designs on the cakes.

Paste food colors create vibrant colored frostings and do not thin the frosting like liquid colorings.

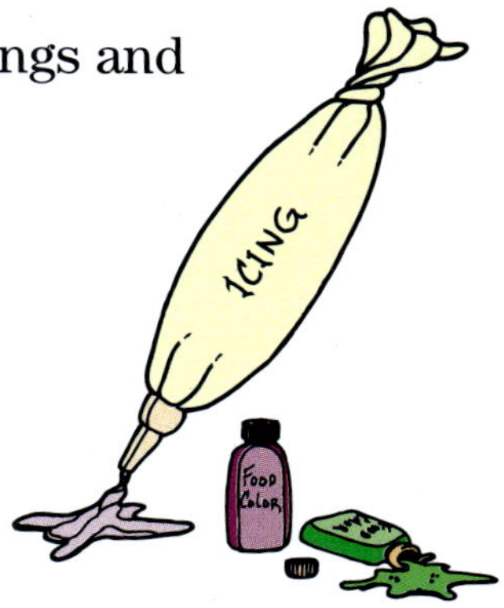

Decorating bags are essential for piping decorations. Make sure you have a bag for each color of frosting.

Decorating tips are used to pipe different shapes. Writing, round and open star tips are the most commonly used tips.

A **coupler** inserted into the pastry bag before filling makes changing tips easier.

Cake boards are made of heavy corrugated cardboard that can be covered and cut to fit the cake shape.

A **pastry brush** is used to remove crumbs from unfrosted cakes.

Cake Basics

BASIC CAKE KNOW-HOW

The perfect cake for decorating is firm, moist and not crumbly. A freshly baked cake can be difficult to work with so plan to bake the cake one day before you need to decorate it. If time doesn't permit, place the cooled cake in the freezer for 30 to 45 minutes to make it easier to cut, frost and decorate.

The Best Baking Pans

Use shiny metal pans or pans with a nonstick finish. Grease and flour all pans before adding the cake batter.

Dividing the Batter

When baking layer cakes, it is important to divide the batter equally to make even layers. Either measure the batter and divide it equally or weigh the pans after adding the batter. Spread the batter evenly and tap the pans on the countertop to remove air bubbles before baking.

Testing for Doneness

Always bake cakes at the oven temperature and for the time specified in the recipe. Test cakes after the shortest time given. A cake is done when a toothpick inserted into the center comes out clean. It should pull away from the sides of the pan and spring back when lightly touched in the center.

Cooling Cakes

Let cakes cool in the pans on wire racks for about 10 minutes. Loosen cake edges with a spatula. Place the rack, top side down, over the pan. Flip the rack and the pan over together and the cake should drop out onto the rack. If it does not come out, tap the bottom of the pan. The cake should come out easily. Remove the pan. Place a second wire rack over the cake and flip both racks and the cake back over so the cake can cool top side up. Remove the top rack. Always cool a cake completely before frosting.

Storing Cakes

Cool cakes completely before covering or storing. If using the undecorated

layers within two days, wrap tightly in foil or plastic wrap and store in a cool place. For longer storage, wrap in plastic wrap, then in heavy-duty foil or place in resealable freezer bags; freeze for up to two months. To thaw, remove the layers from the freezer and let them thaw, wrapped, at room temperature.

BEFORE FROSTING

Covering Cake Boards

Cake boards can be covered with foil, greaseproof paper, paper doilies or plastic wrap. To cover, cut the foil or paper 1 to 2 inches larger than the board. Center the board on the reverse side of the paper. Cut slashes in the paper almost to the board along any curved edges. Fold the edges over the board and tape into place. If a cake is very heavy, stack two cake boards together before covering for additional support.

When you are ready to frost the cake, tuck strips of waxed paper underneath the bottom cake layer to keep the plate or covered board clean. When decorating is complete, carefully slide out the strips and touch up frosting as needed.

Trimming Cakes

If the tops of the cake layers are rounded, trimming them gives more professional results. Use a serrated knife long enough to cut across the top in one stroke, such as a bread knife. Use a gentle sawing motion as you cut through the cake.

The sides of square or rectangular cakes should also be trimmed to make them more even. Use a soft pastry brush to remove all loose cake crumbs.

Cut-Apart Cakes

For cleaner cutting lines and fewer crumbs, place the cake in the freezer for 30 to 45 minutes. Use the diagrams and photos as guides and follow the directions carefully. A ruler and toothpicks are helpful to mark designs and act as guides while cutting.

Frosting Tips

Frosting Consistency
The proper frosting consistency is the secret to successful decorating. Frosting should hold its shape when scooped with a spatula. If the frosting is too soft because the kitchen is warm, refrigerate the frosting for about 15 minutes and keep it chilled while you work. If the frosting is soft because liquid coloring was used or too much milk was added, beat in some additional sifted powdered sugar. If the frosting is too stiff, beat in additional milk, a small amount at a time, until the desired consistency is achieved.

Base Frosting
Frosting cakes with a base frosting (page 3) is a professional technique that gives the cake a smoother, cleaner finish and makes frosting the cake much easier. Spread a thin layer of base frosting on all sides of the cake after cutting and positioning the layers or pieces. Let the base frosting dry a few minutes before covering it with a thicker layer of final frosting.

Frosting Cut-Apart Cakes
Frosting the pointed pieces of cut-up cakes takes extra care. First, freeze the pointed pieces for at least 30 minutes. If frosting a small piece, hold the piece in your hand. Starting at the point, carefully spread thinned frosting along the side, using long strokes away from the point until all sides are frosted. Frost again with thicker frosting. If the tip of the point needs additional frosting, carefully dab it on with the spatula.

Tinting Frosting
To get bright colors and to keep the frosting at the proper consistency, tint frosting with paste food colorings. Add a small amount of the paste color with a toothpick, then stir well. Slowly add more color until the frosting is the desired shade. If you use liquid food coloring and your frosting becomes too thin, add additional powdered sugar, beating until the desired consistency is reached.

Tinting Coconut
Place coconut in resealable plastic food storage bag. Mix a few drops of food coloring with ½ teaspoon water. Add to coconut and close bag. Shake until coconut is evenly coated. Repeat procedure for a darker shade.

Decorating Techniques

DECORATING TIP TECHNIQUES

Using a Decorating Bag

Some recipes call for piped designs. For each of the techniques, you'll need a decorating bag fitted with the appropriate tip and filled with frosting. If you will be using different tips when decorating, a coupler must be used when changing tips. A coupler is used to attach tips to the decorating bag and allows you to change tips without removing the frosting from the bag. To use, unscrew the ring. Insert the cone-shaped piece into the narrow end of an empty decorating bag until the narrow end extends slightly beyond the end of the bag (snip off the end of the decorating bag if necessary). Place the coupler ring over the decorating tip. Screw the ring on to hold the tip in place. To change tips, unscrew the ring, remove the tip, replace with the new tip and screw the ring back in place.

To fill a decorating bag, insert the decorating tip or attach the tip with a coupler. Fold the top of the bag down, then use a spatula to place the frosting in the bag. In general, fill the bag half to two-thirds full, then unfold the top of the bag. Twist the top of the bag tightly against the frosting.

Place twisted end of the bag in the palm of your writing hand. Position fingers near the opening of the bag. Position other hand under bag to guide tip as shown.

When piping, hold the bag so the tip is at the angle indicated for the technique. Then, gently squeeze to force the frosting out, using even pressure while guiding the tip. Do not loosen your grip on the twisted end or the frosting will begin to push up and out of the top of the bag. Push mainly with the palm of your hand rather than squeezing with your fingers.

Decorating Techniques

Line (use writing or small open star tip): Hold bag so tip is at a 45° angle to the right. While gently squeezing bag, guide tip opening just above cake in a straight, curved, zigzag or squiggly line. To end line, stop squeezing, then lift tip.

Writing (use writing tip): Hold bag so tip is at a 45° angle to the right for horizontal lines and toward you for vertical lines. While gently squeezing bag, guide tip opening just above cake to form print or script letters. Stop squeezing, then lift tip at the end of each letter for print letters and at the end of each word for script writing. To pipe built up writing, start piping letter and then hesitate briefly while still squeezing. When desired amount of frosting has built up, resume gliding tip opening for letter. Try to evenly space the built up areas on the letters.

Dot (use round tip): Hold bag so tip is at a 90° angle. Position opening just above the cake and gently squeeze. Lift slightly while still squeezing. When dot is desired size, stop squeezing, then lift tip. To pipe a dot border, position tip almost touching first dot and pipe another dot. Repeat to complete border.

Star (use open or closed star tip): Hold bag so tip is at a 90° angle. Position opening just above cake and gently squeeze. Lift slightly while still squeezing. When star is desired size, stop squeezing, then lift tip. To pipe a star border, position tip almost touching first star and pipe another star. Repeat to complete border.

Cookie Dough Basics

GENERAL GUIDELINES

- Measure all the ingredients and assemble them in the order called for in the recipe.
- All cookie dough should be well chilled before using. Unless the recipe states otherwise, work with the recommended portion of dough called for and refrigerate the remaining dough until needed.
- Follow recipe directions and baking times. Check for doneness using the test given in the recipe.
- Most refrigerated cookie dough expands considerably when baked. Always leave two inches between cookies when placing them on cookie sheets.

SPECIAL TECHNIQUES

Making Patterns:
When a pattern is to be used only once, make the pattern out of waxed paper. Using the diagram(s) and photo as guides, draw the pattern pieces on waxed paper. Cut the pieces out and place them on the rolled-out dough. Cut around the pattern pieces with a sharp knife. Remove the pattern pieces and discard. Continue as directed in the recipe.

For patterns that are used more than once, make the pattern more durable by using clean lightweight cardboard or poster board. Using the diagram(s) and photo as guides, draw the pattern pieces on the cardboard. Cut the pieces out and lightly spray one side with nonstick cooking spray. Place the pattern pieces, sprayed side down, on the rolled-out dough and cut around them with a sharp knife. Reuse the pattern pieces to make as many cutouts as needed.

Cookie Dough Basics

Melting Chocolate:
When melting chocolate be sure the utensils are completely dry. Any drop of moisture makes the chocolate become stiff and grainy. If this does happen, add 1⁄2 teaspoon shortening (not butter) for each ounce of chocolate and stir until smooth. Chocolate scorches easily, and once scorched cannot be used. Use one of the following three methods for successful melting.

Double Boiler: Place the chocolate in the top of a double boiler or in a heatproof bowl over hot, not boiling, water. Stir until smooth. (Make sure the water remains just below a simmer and is one inch below the top pan.) Be careful that no steam or water gets into the chocolate.

Direct Heat: Place the chocolate in a heavy saucepan and melt over very low heat, stirring constantly. Remove the chocolate from the heat as soon as it is melted. Be sure to watch the chocolate carefully since it is easily scorched with this method.

Microwave Oven: Place a 1-ounce square of chocolate or 1 cup of chocolate chips in a small microwavable bowl. Microwave at HIGH 1 to 2 minutes or until the chocolate is almost melted, stirring well after every minute. Add 10 seconds for each additional ounce of chocolate. Be sure to stir the microwaved chocolate well because it retains its original shape even when melted.

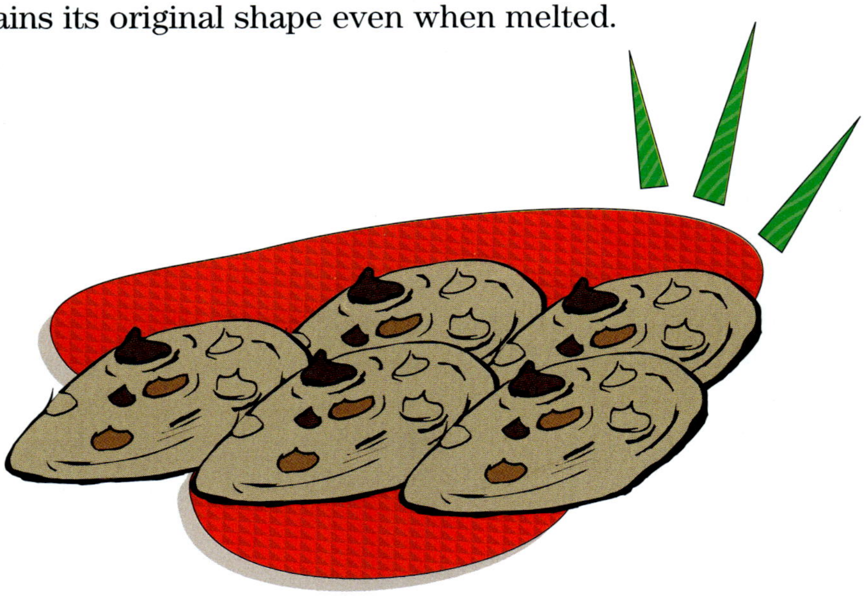

General Substitutions

If you don't have:	Use:
1 teaspoon baking powder	½ teaspoon baking soda plus ¼ teaspoon cream of tartar
½ cup firmly packed brown sugar	½ cup sugar mixed with 2 tablespoons molasses
1 cup buttermilk	1 tablespoon lemon juice or vinegar plus milk to equal 1 cup (stir; let stand 5 minutes)
1 ounce (1 square) unsweetened baking chocolate	3 tablespoons unsweetened cocoa plus 1 tablespoon shortening
3 ounces (3 squares) semisweet baking chocolate	3 ounces (½ cup) semisweet chocolate morsels
1 whole egg	2 egg yolks plus 1 teaspoon cold water
1 cup cake flour	1 cup minus 2 tablespoons all-purpose flour
1 cup honey	1¼ cups granulated sugar plus ¼ cup water

Common Weights and Measures

½ tablespoon = 1½ teaspoons	½ pint = 1 cup or 8 fluid ounces
1 tablespoon = 3 teaspoons	1 pint = 2 cups or 16 fluid ounces
¼ cup = 4 tablespoons	1 quart = 4 cups or 2 pints or 32 fluid ounces
⅓ cup = 5 tablespoons plus 1 teaspoon	1 gallon = 16 cups or 4 quarts
½ cup = 8 tablespoons	1 pound = 16 ounces

Metric Conversion Chart

VOLUME MEASUREMENTS (dry)

1/8 teaspoon = 0.5 mL
1/4 teaspoon = 1 mL
1/2 teaspoon = 2 mL
3/4 teaspoon = 4 mL
1 teaspoon = 5 mL
1 tablespoon = 15 mL
2 tablespoons = 30 mL
1/4 cup = 60 mL
1/3 cup = 75 mL
1/2 cup = 125 mL
2/3 cup = 150 mL
3/4 cup = 175 mL
1 cup = 250 mL
2 cups = 1 pint = 500 mL
3 cups = 750 mL
4 cups = 1 quart = 1 L

VOLUME MEASUREMENTS (fluid)

1 fluid ounce (2 tablespoons) = 30 mL
4 fluid ounces (1/2 cup) = 125 mL
8 fluid ounces (1 cup) = 250 mL
12 fluid ounces (1 1/2 cups) = 375 mL
16 fluid ounces (2 cups) = 500 mL

WEIGHTS (mass)

1/2 ounce = 15 g
1 ounce = 30 g
3 ounces = 90 g
4 ounces = 120 g
8 ounces = 225 g
10 ounces = 285 g
12 ounces = 360 g
16 ounces = 1 pound = 450 g

DIMENSIONS

1/16 inch = 2 mm
1/8 inch = 3 mm
1/4 inch = 6 mm
1/2 inch = 1.5 cm
3/4 inch = 2 cm
1 inch = 2.5 cm

OVEN TEMPERATURES

250°F = 120°C
275°F = 140°C
300°F = 150°C
325°F = 160°C
350°F = 180°C
375°F = 190°C
400°F = 200°C
425°F = 220°C
450°F = 230°C

BAKING PAN SIZES

Utensil	Size in Inches/Quarts	Metric Volume	Size in Centimeters
Baking or Cake Pan (square or rectangular)	8×8×2	2 L	20×20×5
	9×9×2	2.5 L	23×23×5
	12×8×2	3 L	30×20×5
	13×9×2	3.5 L	33×23×5
Loaf Pan	8×4×3	1.5 L	20×10×7
	9×5×3	2 L	23×13×7
Round Layer Cake Pan	8×1½	1.2 L	20×4
	9×1½	1.5 L	23×4
Pie Plate	8×1¼	750 mL	20×3
	9×1¼	1 L	23×3
Baking Dish or Casserole	1 quart	1 L	—
	1½ quart	1.5 L	—
	2 quart	2 L	—

Acknowledgments

The publisher would like to thank the companies and organizations listed below for the use of their recipes and photographs in this publication.

Bestfoods
Bob Evans®
Campbell Soup Company
ConAgra Grocery Products Company
Dole Food Company, Inc.
Duncan Hines® and Moist Deluxe® are registered trademarks of Aurora Foods Inc.
Egg Beaters®
The Golden Grain Company®
Hershey Foods Corporation
Hormel Foods Corporation
The HV Company
Kraft Foods, Inc.
Land O'Lakes, Inc.
Lawry's® Foods, Inc.
Lipton®
M&M/MARS
National Honey Board
Nestlé USA, Inc.
OREO® Cookies
The Procter & Gamble Company
Reckitt Benckiser
The J.M. Smucker Company
StarKist® Seafood Company
Texas Peanut Producers Board
Uncle Ben's Inc.

Index

Index

Index

Index

Index